AWAKEN THE FORCE

Unleash your Quantum Consciousness

JC Gordon

Hidden Lighthouse Publishers
http://fullservicepublishing.wordpress.com

Email: fullservicepublishing@yahoo.ca

© 2015 JC Gordon
All rights reserved.

No part of this book may be used or reproduced in any manner whatsoever without written permission except in the case of brief quotation.

Cover design, page design and composition by Corey Van leperen
Illustrations by Corey Van leperen www.corycatures.com

Awaken the Force: Unleash your Quantum Consciousness
First Edition

© 2015 JC Gordon
All rights reserved.

ISBN 978-1502801234

In loving memory of my adopted parents

Merle and Willard, and my father,

Bob McNair.

To my wonderful wife Ella, thank you for your friendship,

support, love and continued encouragement.

You are the GREATEST!

To my dear friends Dorothy Ramsey,

Ed and Hope Rychkun, Mike Desrochers, & Paul Jackson,

thank you for the strength and

support.

My hope is you choose to

unleash your Quantum Consciousness

and limitless potential.

Contents

PART 1: The Journey

1. My Experience 7

PART 2: The Blueprint

2. The Revealing 19
3. The First Energy Seal 26
4. The Second Energy Seal 29
5. The Third Energy Seal 32
6. The Fourth Energy Seal 38
7. The Fifth Energy Seal 40
8. The Sixth Energy Seal 44
9. The Seventh Energy Seal 47
10. The Eighth Energy Seal 50
11. The Ninth Energy Seal 53
12. The Tenth Energy Seal 56

PART 3: Today's 70 Year Transformation

13. Energy 61
14. Transfiguration 72
15. Changing Your Energetic Disposition 80

16. The Illusion 100

17. Activations of Transformation 127

18. Super Humanity 158

19. The Hundredth Monkey Tipping Point 182

20. The Final Days 187

PART 4: The Ascension

21. Lift Off 195

PART 5: The After Life

22. Forever 207

PART 6: The Choice

23. The Crossroads of Time 213

Glossary 225

Part 1

The Journey

1

My Experience

"Let your heart feel for the infliction and distress of everyone."

George Washington

Looking back on your life, I'm sure you can recall the day that impacted you the most.

For me it was June 25, 1996. I was living near Hagensborg, British Columbia, Canada. It started off as a normal day until 1:10 in the afternoon. At this moment I was cutting wood using a chainsaw when suddenly it kicked back and nearly decapitated me. It sliced the left side of my throat wide open from my jawbone to my collarbone. I remember looking down and seeing my white sweatshirt turn blood red.

With the chainsaw still on and stuck to my sweatshirt against my chest, I intuitively heard a wee small voice from within tell me *"Everything will be OK, I have a purpose for your life."* It was the inspiration I needed to get me through what was to come.

It was amazing how this inspiration just calmed me down as I had absolutely no panic. I hollered at Young Kim who was working with me and motioned for him to come and help.

When he saw what happened he sprinted over to me. In his broken Korean- English he asked "What to do, what to do." I told him "turn the chainsaw off".

I had a very old chainsaw that 19 times out of 20 did not work when its red kill switch was pushed, but fortunately this time it did. Young Kim turned the chainsaw off and pulled it off of me.

I told Young Kim to go and get Steve. Steve Johnson was driving an excavator about fifty yards away. Young Kim ran and told Steve what happened. I remember Steve turning around to see what Young Kim was talking about. When he realized what had happened he immediately jumped down from his excavator and sprinted to me.

Fortunately nothing rattled Steve; he calmly took my arm and led me to his truck and told Young Kim to call 9-1-1 right away.

I was about 45 minutes from the nearest hospital in Bella Coola. The Bella Coola Hospital is nothing more than a medical outpost. There is only one paved road in the Bella Coola valley. About twenty minutes into driving towards the hospital Steve and I saw the ambulance speeding towards us on the other side of the road with its lights flashing. I remember Steve rolled down his window and waved the ambulance down. The ambulance stopped, made a u-turn and pulled in behind us at the side of the road.

Steve told me to wait in the truck while he went and spoke with the ambulance attendants. After about thirty seconds I decided to get up and walk over to meet them at the back of the ambulance. When the ambulance attendant saw me her eyes opened wide like she had just seen a dead man walking. She immediately helped me into the back of the ambulance.

The ambulance ride to the Bella Coola Hospital was another 25 minutes. During the ride the ambulance attendant asked me 8 times what my name was fearing I was about to pass out and die on her. Finally when she asked me the final time I was impressed to tell her "Don't worry everything will be fine". She now thought for sure I was delirious and ready to die.

The hospital staff had been notified that the ambulance was bringing me in and they were prepared for my arrival. I remember being moved into the Bella Coola Hospital emergency room on the ambulance stretcher.

The Bella Coola Hospital had 3 doctors who rotated shifts and on this day one of the doctors was away on vacation. Fortunately, he had been replaced by a retired locum from Saltspring Island. He was the only one of the 3 who had the confidence and ability to stitch me up. While lying on my back the doctor was on my left and his nurse was on my right.

I remember the nurse showed the doctor an antiseptic in a sealed packet and asked him if she should use it. I recall the doctor did not know what she was holding; he leaned over me to get a closer look at the packet and asked the nurse "What the hell is that?" When she told him what she was holding he said "Yeah yeah put it on." The nurse proceeded to open the packet and rubbed its contents on my wound to make sure any germs and microorganisms were killed and no infection would spread.

Next, I remember the doctor attempting to thread the eye of his needle with suture thread. He tried several times threading his needle's eye with the suture thread but finally handed it over in frustration to the nurse after he could not thread it. His needle looked exactly like a fishing hook. I said out loud when he passed his needle "It's all good everything will be fine." The nurse easily threaded his needle with the suture thread and handed it back to the doctor.

The next thing I knew I was no longer in my body, I was separated from it. I was suddenly floating at the ceiling of the emergency room looking down at myself lying on the stretcher. The doctor was now on my right and the nurse was now on my left. I remember seeing the tops of their heads. I saw my neck sliced wide open; it looked like raw meat with blood everywhere.

11 / AWAKEN THE FORCE

Suddenly the doctor started moving his needle towards my wound. Just as it touched me I left the emergency room.

I was now in what I can best describe as a pitch black elevator. There was a slight vibration but no noise. I sensed I was moving through the cosmos of time in an upward direction. I looked up and saw a small twinkling light. At first, the light was like a star in the sky. Suddenly it began to get larger. It gradually became an all encompassing white light that I passed through.

As I moved through the white light I had an overwhelming sense of security, I knew I was home. I sensed wherever this was; it is where I am supposed to be and where I wanted to be. There was an absolute peace about passing through the white light and I certainly did not want to leave wherever it was I was at.

I landed on a meadow at the top of a very high mountain. The grass was growing wild, the sunlight was magnificent and there were no clouds in the brilliant blue sky. I could see forever in every direction. Suddenly a force began guiding me; it gently touched me in what I perceived was my left elbow. However, I had no body.

I floated down the mountain following a pathway without any cares or concerns. I did not know where I was going but knew I was in a very special place. In the distance I saw a magnificent, sparkling, temple like structure. It was centered in a very large walled, gated property. As I approached the wall its large wooden gate automatically opened for me. As I entered the property I floated past the open gate and was guided towards the temple.

Nearing the temple its front doors swung open, backwards from the left and from the right. I entered the temple. Inside there was no sign of life but energetically it felt very peaceful and comforting. I was led to the stairway on the right. The temple's walls were made of what looked like cut stone. The stones were all the same size and had the same rectangular cut. As I moved up the stairway, there was no handrail on the left; on my right was the stone wall.

When I reached the top of the stairway, I turned left and made my way down a hallway as there was no place to go on the right. First, I went past a room on the left whose door was open. The room was barren except for 4 entities who were sitting on the floor. I sensed they were praying or meditating. I could not make out any discernible features on them. I continued down the hallway and next saw a room on the right with an open door. There was no life in this room as it was only a vast library of books. I went down the hallway a little further and entered the next doorway on the right. I entered the room and sensed the door close behind me.

I then began to experience a warmth and presence that morphed into a radiant cloud of countless particles. It was like the snow on a TV screen. For a split second, I remember seeing the face of my deceased maternal grandfather in the radiant cloud and then I saw the image change into the face of another older male I had never seen before.

Suddenly, 6 violet colored dots appeared around the radiant cloud in a perfect sequence. The first violet colored dot appeared at 1 o'clock. The second violet color dot appeared at 3 o'clock to the right of the radiant cloud. The third violet colored dot appeared at 5 o'clock. The fourth violet colored dot appeared at 7 o'clock below the radiant cloud. The fifth violet colored dot appeared at 9 o'clock and the sixth violet colored dot appeared at 11 o'clock above the radiant cloud.

The 6 violet colored dots were energy centers that came alive and became a brilliant violet color. Then, the 6 energy centers began to unleash violet lightning energy that looked like moving fingers. The violet lightning energy moving fingers connected with the 6 energy centers to create one solid violet energy connection. At this moment the violet energy centers began communicating with me.

The communication was neither verbal nor audible. It was energetic through violet energy zings that were like bolts of lightning that just kept zinging me between the eyes. It was like I was in a game of laser tag.

I was zinged that I was with the thoughts of God and in the inner workings of God's mind. It was like meeting someone for the first time and being able to go into their mind and watch their thought process of how and what they are thinking. My violet energy zings were from the Quantum Consciousness of God. They did not hurt; in fact I did not recall feeling anything from them. They revealed the energetic thoughts of God's Quantum Consciousness.

I was in awe and experienced a heightened level of inspiration and peace as I knew I had been here many times before. Whenever the violet energy zings of God's Quantum Consciousness hit me from all 6 violet energy centers at the same time the interior radiant cloud would turn on to reveal live images from within it like a computer or television screen.

I did not want my experience with God's Quantum Consciousness to end as it revealed to me its energetic perfection and perfect love meaning for life. However, much to my regret the Quantum Consciousness of God's final violet energy zing informed me that I *"must return so all is fulfilled."*

When the communication ended, the Quantum Consciousness of God began to slowly decrease its intensity until it disappeared. Then its energy centers were turned off. Finally the radiant cloud in the middle disappeared. Lastly the warmth and energy of the force was gone. At this moment my new life began.

The door behind me opened; I turned and exited the room. I moved in the opposite direction along the hallway, again being led by the same force that guided me when I arrived. I went down the stairway that was now on my right.

At the bottom of the stairway I turned right again as I was now back on the main level. I exited the temple through the doorway, after the front doors again automatically opened for me. I slowly moved through the property. As I approached the great wall its large wooden gate again automatically opened and I exited through it.

I was moving in the opposite direction from which I had come. I began to move up the mountainside. When I reached the mountaintop I immediately saw a rabbit hole and knew I needed to go down it.

Through the rabbit hole I began travelling downward in the pitch black elevator through the cosmos of time. Suddenly, I was back in the Bella Coola Hospital emergency room. I remember seeing everybody frantically scramble about. I saw the doctor, the nurse and a handful of unrecognizable others.

I slowly floated down from the emergency room ceiling back into my body. I remember opening my eyes and looking straight into the doctor's eyes that were directly over me about 6 inches away.

When I opened my eyes, I remember he calmly shouted to everybody "It's ok, he's back."

Part 2

The Blueprint

2

The Revealing

The Bella Coola Hospital staff nicknamed me the 'miracle man' for surviving death. However, the real miracle was what the Quantum Consciousness of God revealed to me during my near death experience or NDE.

The Quantum Consciousness of God is its violet energy force of energetic perfection and perfect love. It is the energetic mastermind plan of life that is regulated through energy. Energy is the regulator and energetic pulse of Quantum Consciousness that has been perfectly orchestrated everywhere at every moment into everything to energetically complete God's Quantum Consciousness mastermind plan of life.

My NDE revealed that God is asexual. The male aspect of God is its mind and violet energy force of Quantum Consciousness. The female aspect of God is its energetic womb where life has been energetically conceived into existence through God's violet energy force of Quantum Consciousness.

During my NDE, the male aspect and Quantum Consciousness of God inspired me through its continuous violet energy zings and the female aspect of God revealed to me what was within its inner energetic womb that God's Quantum Consciousness had energetically thought into existence. The violet energy zings from God was like watching a fast strobe light. Each zing was an energetic thought of God's Quantum Consciousness. My NDE was divided into two presentations. First was the energetic preview followed by the energetic main attraction.

God's violet energy zings were either individual energy zings from one energy centre or collective energy zings from all 6 energy centers at once. When the collective energy zings happened they would also visually reveal their meaning in life from within God's radiant cloud and energetic womb. When the energetic womb was turned on it was like I had a front row seat at a cinema and was watching a movie.

Quantum Consciousness's first violet energy zings were collective. They revealed an energetic preview from within God's energetic womb and I had the lead starring role in it.

I was about 6 or 7 years old. I remember seeing myself walking on a street that felt familiar but was not recognizable. I then saw myself being gently lifted off of the street I was walking on. I saw myself ascending upwards until the neighborhood around the street became visible.

21 / AWAKEN THE FORCE

I continued my ascension until the neighborhood became a larger city and then suddenly the city disappeared into the planet. My ascension continued until the planet disappeared into the Universe.

At this time I was moving through the Universe at a lightning speed and then suddenly I was outside of the Universe. The Universe appeared as a round dark sphere that gradually began to get smaller and smaller until it became a tiny red light that moved to 9 o'clock in God's energetic womb.

Suddenly another tiny red light appeared below the first red light that was at 9 o'clock in the inner energetic womb and then an infinite amount of red lights appeared. Then they all began to twinkle. They formed a tiny fetus that did not move. I watched as the energetic fetus's red lights grew and took up the complete bottom half of the inner energetic womb.

My attention next moved to a violet sun that was in the top half of the inner energetic womb. When I gazed upon the violet sun it entered the fetus's first twinkling red light. When the violet sun entered the first twinkling red light it immediately transfigured from a red light to a violet light. Then suddenly all of the other twinkling red lights also transfigured into violet lights.

I then saw the upper half of the inner energetic womb become alive. As it came alive it created a 3D circular vortex of light that spiraled in a clockwise direction. Suddenly the violet energetic fetus was pulled into the spiraling 3D vortex rays of sunlight and began moving towards the spiraling vortex of light. The head of the violet energetic fetus entered the vortex and then the rest of the violet energetic fetus followed.

When the violet energetic fetus had completely disappeared the inner energetic womb was barren.

This ended my energetic preview.

It was now time for the energetic main attraction to begin. It began immediately after my energetic preview had ended. It too began with collective energy zings from all 6 energy centers and it visually revealed itself visually from within God's energetic womb. I was inspired that the starring role in the energetic main attraction is the Quantum Consciousness of God. The energetic main attraction began by revealing the energetic foundation of Quantum Consciousness. It is life's Energetic Blueprint.

I was zinged that life's Energetic Blueprint was the initial thought of Quantum Consciousness. It was the ground zero starting point of God's thoughts.

Life's Energetic Blueprint consisted of ten energy seals which represent the energetic milestone event of God's mastermind plan of life.

Below is God's Energetic Blueprint of life.

Energetic Blueprint of life

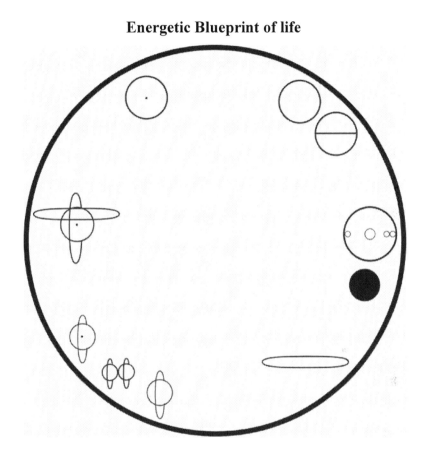

The energy seals of Quantum Consciousness are strategically designed circular seals of authenticity. The circle is simplicity at its finest and the perfect geometric shape for the ten energy seals. The circle represents peace, prosperity, perfection and closure.

The opening of each energy seal created a strand of violet energy Quantum Consciousness. The totality of the 10 violet energy strands is the totality of God's violet energy force of Quantum Consciousness.

The main attraction of my NDE was about to reveal the meaning of life from the perspective of God's Quantum Consciousness.

3

The First Energy Seal

The energetic main attraction of God's Quantum Consciousness now began.

I saw the first energy seal energetically unlock on the Energetic Blueprint of life and was zinged that Quantum Consciousness refers to it as the Alpha seal.

Next I received a collective energy zing that revealed a massive explosion from within God's energetic womb. It came from the blackness of nothing and I was zinged that it took place 13.75 billion years ago. It represented the beginning of life and time.

I later learned that science refers to this explosion as the big bang and spirituality refers to this explosion as the creation of heaven and earth.

It was the physics professor and Belgian priest Georges Lemaitre who in 1927 first theorized the big bang. Lemaitre realized the

Universe was constantly expanding from its infinitely small, dense, starting point that astrophysicists call the singularity. I witnessed the singularity actually happen from the perspective of the Quantum Consciousness of God when Alpha was energetically unlocked.

My next energy zings were also collective and they revealed that the massive explosion began to shrink in size until it became a small twinkling red light that moved to 9 o'clock in the inner energetic womb. When it was positioned at 9 o'clock I then saw a limitless number of other small, twinkling red lights appear below the first red light. They formed a very tiny twinkling red light fetus.

I was zinged that the total number of twinkling red lights which make up the entire energetic fetus of God is 100 trillion. It is the exact number of cells that make up the human body.

I was next zinged that the first red light I saw is our Universe and the other 100 trillion red lights are the multiverse of God's Quantum Consciousness.

I then saw a white lightning bolt strike every twinkling red light. The energy from the white lightning bolt burrowed itself into the 100 trillion red twinkling lights. The energy from the white lightning bolt united with each of the twinkling red lights exactly as sperm unites with the egg to create human life. I later learned that the energy from the white lightning bolt has been identified by science as the strong force of nature.

The energetic unlocking of the Alpha energy seal created the Alpha strand of God's violet energy Quantum Consciousness. This was the violet energy that produced the energetic conception of God's energetic fetus.

4

The Second Energy Seal

With the first violet energy strand of God's Quantum Consciousness complete the second energy seal was energetically unlocked on the Energetic Blueprint of life.

I saw the second energy seal energetically unlock on the Energetic Blueprint of life and was zinged that Quantum Consciousness refers to it as the Beta seal. It was energetically unlocked one second after the energy seal of Alpha was energetically unlocked 13.75 billion years ago.

I saw in the inner energetic womb that when Quantum Consciousness energetically unlocked its Beta energy seal the energetic fetus became alive and grew ever so slightly. I was zinged that this growth was from the release of the energy from the white lightning bolt at the opening of the Alpha energy seal one second earlier as it burrowed itself into the 100 trillion twinkling red lights and energetic cells of God's energetic fetus.

The 100 trillion energetic cell fetus of God grew ever so slightly at the opening of its Beta energy seal because the strong force of nature was binding protons and neutrons together to form the nucleus of every atom in every energetic cell. It was the forming of every atom's nucleus in all 100 trillion energetic cells of God's energetic fetus that caused the energetic fetus of God to grow when the second energy seal was unlocked.

I remember next seeing in the top half of God's inner energetic womb a violet sun. I watched as it began to move freely around. I was zinged that this is the violet energy Quantum Consciousness of God.

I was further zinged that the lower half of the inner energetic womb is our physical realm and the top half of the inner energetic womb is our spiritual realm.

Quantum Consciousness then zinged me with the energetic differences between the physical realm and the spiritual realm. The zings inspired me that physical realm energy cannot exist in the spiritual realm; however spiritual realm energy exists in both the spiritual and physical realms.

I next saw in the inner energetic womb a red lightning bolt from the violet sun strike every twinkling red light and energy cell of

God. The energy from it also burrowed itself into the 100 trillion red twinkling lights and energy cells exactly as sperm unites with the egg to create human life. I later learned that the energy from the red lightning bolt has been identified by science as the electromagnetic force of nature.

The energetic unlocking of the Beta energy seal created the Beta strand of God's violet energy Quantum Consciousness. This was the violet energy that began the energetic gestation of God's energetic fetus.

5

The Third Energy Seal

With the second violet energy strand of God's Quantum Consciousness complete the third energy seal was energetically unlocked on the Energetic Blueprint of life.

I saw the third energy seal energetically unlock on the Energetic Blueprint of life and was zinged that Quantum Consciousness refers to it as the Gamma seal. It was energetically unlocked one second after the energy seal of Beta was energetically unlocked and two seconds after the energy seal of Alpha was energetically unlocked 13.75 billion years ago.

I saw in the inner energetic womb when Quantum Consciousness energetically unlocked its Gamma energy seal the energetic fetus of God again became alive and grew ever so slightly. I was zinged that this growth was from the release of the energy from the red lightning bolt at the energetic unlocking of the Beta energy seal one second earlier as it burrowed itself into the 100 trillion twinkling red lights and energetic cells of God's energetic fetus. The 100 trillion energetic cell fetus of God grew ever so slightly at the opening of its Gamma energy seal because the accelerating expansion of all the atoms in all its 100 trillion energetic cells was pulled together by the electromagnetic force.

After the 100 trillion energetic cell fetus of God grew I saw 4 tiny violet circular windows appear in the inner energetic womb. I was zinged that these windows are energetic portals where Quantum Consciousness transitions itself back and forth between the spiritual realm and the physical realm.

The first circular window appeared on the outer edges of the inner energetic womb at 9 o'clock. It energetically connects the top spiritual realm with the lower physical realm. I was zinged that this window is the birth portal between the spiritual realm and the physical realm. I was further zinged that this is where our souls and violet energy threads of Quantum Consciousness transition themselves from the spiritual realm to the physical realm.

The second circular window appeared on the outer edges of the inner energetic womb at 3 o'clock. It too energetically connected the top spiritual realm with the lower physical realm. It was the same size as the first window. When it appeared I was zinged that this circular window is the death portal between the physical realm and the spiritual realm. I was zinged that this is where our souls and violet energy threads of Quantum Consciousness transition themselves back to the spiritual realm from the physical realm.

The third circular window appeared directly beside the second circular window at 3 o'clock in the inner energetic womb. It also energetically connected the top spiritual realm with the lower physical realm. It was the same size as the first and second circular windows. I was zinged that this circular window is the near death portal between the physical realm and the spiritual realm. I was further zinged that this energetic portal is where the souls and the violet energy threads of Quantum Consciousness transition themselves from the physical realm to the spiritual realm.

The fourth and final circular window appeared in the middle of the inner energetic womb. It too energetically connected the top spiritual realm with the lower physical realm. I saw this energetic portal was noticeably larger than the first, second and third energetic portals and was the exact same size as the violet sun that moved about in the upper white half of the inner energetic womb. I was zinged this energetic portal is for the violet energy totality of Quantum Consciousness.

I next saw in the inner energetic womb a black lightning bolt from the violet sun strike every twinkling red light and energy cell of God. The energy from the black lightning bolt also burrowed itself into the 100 trillion red twinkling lights and energy cells exactly as sperm unites with the egg to create human life. I later learned that the energy from the black lightning bolt has been identified by science as gravity. The black lightning bolt of gravity not only applies to objects it also applies to the gravitational force of energy. Many physicists have postulated about science's fifth force of nature which is our soul's gravitational force. This was also unleashed through the black lightning bolt.

Souls are not a physical part of our bodies, rather they are the energetic essence of who we are and without them our cells have no energy and are dead. Our souls are violet energy threads of Quantum Consciousness that energetically transition themselves back and forth between the spiritual realm and the physical realm and the physical realm and the spiritual realm.

After I died it was my soul and violet energy thread of Quantum Consciousness that entered its gravitational force. Every soul enters its gravitational force when it removes itself either at the death of or near death of the body it had been in.

My NDE revealed that when the soul leaves the body during its NDE it is exactly the same as when the soul leaves the body at death except it is energetically filtered through the near death portal rather than the death portal.

The soul and violet energy thread of Quantum Consciousness after death or near death of the person it has resided in leaves the body and enters the soul's gravitational force. It energetically crosses out of the physical realm into the spiritual realm through either the death or near death portal. The soul's gravitational force can only affect the soul once it leaves the physical body. When a person is alive the soul cannot enter its gravitational force because it is in the body.

I was zinged next about how the soul's gravitational force works. Once the soul has been filtered out the spiritual realm through the birth portal it then enters the soul's gravitational force and is energetically transitioned to the physical realm from the spiritual realm. The soul's gravitational force guides the soul to its physical realm re-entry point which is its predetermined female terminus it has been predestined to enter.

The re-entry of the soul into its predestined female terminus produces the female's ovulation. It is the energetic wisdom of the soul and Quantum Consciousness of God to either accept or deny conception based upon its predetermined purpose. If the energetic circumstances are favorable for the soul to carry out its life energy contract's predetermined purpose then conception takes place. If the energetic circumstances are not favorable for the soul to carry out its life energy contract's predetermined purpose the soul will not energetically allow conception to take place.

The first step of all souls as they reenter the physical realm is to energetically burrow themselves into the hypothalamus of their predestined female terminus. The hypothalamus is a portion of the brain which contains a number of small nuclei which have a variety of functions. The hypothalamus triggers the anterior lobe of the pituitary gland to release the follicle-stimulating hormone which produces a female's ovulation.

It is impossible for the fields of mathematics, probability and statistics to calculate the chances of every single person who has ever walked the face of the earth, having for the most part, the same 100 trillion cells. It is not random chance this has happened. It has happened because at conception our souls energetically move into the ovum of their predestined female terminus to carry out their energetic instructions of Quantum Consciousness for the segmentation process to fully develop the fetus until birth.

When the fetus is fully developed by way of the souls energetic instructions from the Quantum Consciousness of God, the fetus and soul are birthed into the physical realm.

The energetic unlocking of the Gamma energy seal created the Gamma strand of God's violet energy Quantum Consciousness. This was the violet energy that continued the energetic gestation of God's energetic fetus.

6

The Fourth Energy Seal

With the third violet energy strand of God's Quantum Consciousness complete the fourth energy seal was energetically unlocked on the Energetic Blueprint of life.

I saw the fourth energy seal energetically unlock on the Energetic Blueprint of life and was zinged that Quantum Consciousness refers to it as the Delta seal. It was energetically unlocked one second after the energy seal of Gamma was energetically unlocked, two seconds after the energy seal of Beta was energetically unlocked and three seconds after the energy seal of Alpha was energetically unlocked 13.75 billion years ago.

I saw in the inner energetic womb that when Quantum Consciousness energetically unlocked its Delta energy seal the energetic fetus became alive and again grew ever so slightly. I was zinged that this growth was from the release of the energy from the black lightning bolt of gravity at the unlocking of the Gamma energy seal one second earlier as it burrowed itself into the 100 trillion twinkling red lights and energetic cells of God's energetic fetus.

I next saw in the inner energetic womb a pale lightning bolt from the violet sun strike every twinkling red light and energy cell of God. The energy from the pale lightning bolt also burrowed itself into the 100 trillion red twinkling lights and energy cells exactly as sperm unites with the egg to create human life. I later learned that the energy from the pale lightning bolt has been identified by science as the weak force of nature which changes the identity of particles through force carriers that operate at distances of about 0.1% of a protons diameter. The weak force of nature changes atoms into entirely new elements when they become very close to each other. The energy from the pale lightning bolt also unleashed the energetic power that would control and manipulate humanity.

The energetic unlocking of the Delta energy seal created the Delta strand of God's violet energy Quantum Consciousness. This was the violet energy of endurance during the energetic gestation of God's energetic fetus.

7

The Fifth Energy Seal

With the fourth violet energy strand of God's Quantum Consciousness complete the fifth energy seal was energetically unlocked on the Energetic Blueprint of life.

I saw the fifth energy seal energetically unlock on the Energetic Blueprint of life and was zinged that Quantum Consciousness refers to it as the Epsilon seal. It was energetically unlocked on December 21, 2012 at 11:11:11 GMT, 13.75 billion years after the energetic unlocking of the fourth energy seal.

I saw in the inner energetic womb that when Epsilon was unlocked the energetic fetus of God was now full term in size and took up the complete lower half of the inner energetic womb. God's energetic fetus had now completed its 13.75 billion year gestation.

I next saw the violet sun of God's violet energy Quantum Consciousness transition out of the spiritual realm through its energetic portal into its first red light energy cell and our Universe.

Upon returning after my NDE I learned that 5000 years ago one of the most advanced civilizations on the planet was the Maya.

The Maya were not only known for their fully developed written language, but also for their art, architecture, mathematical and astronomical systems. The knowledge and wisdom of the Maya produced an advanced time forecasting devise that revealed the moment in time when the unlocking of the Epsilon energy seal would take place.

The Maya's advanced time forecasting devise was known as their 5,126 year long cycle Mesoamerican Long Count calendar. The end of their calendar foretold the exact moment in time when a new era of significant positive physical and spiritual transformational benefits for earth and its inhabitants would occur. The time of the end of the Maya's 5,126 year long cycle Mesoamerican Long Count calendar was December 21, 2012 at 11:11:11 GMT. This was the exact moment in time when the Epsilon energetic seal was energetically unlocked and the violet energy Quantum Consciousness of God transitioned out of the spiritual realm into the physical realm.

John Perkins, a former chief economist at a major international consulting firm and New York Times best-selling author of *Confessions of an Economic Hit Man and Hoodwinked* wrote about the Maya understanding about December 21, 2012 this way: *"Although there are many different interpretations of this prophecy, the one most widely accepted by the Maya teachers I know is taken from the Popul Vuh, the Mayan creation myth. Far from predicting a Hollywood-style doomsday, it holds out the possibility of positive transformation. In its simplest form, the people overthrow an egotistical regime characterized by exploitation and deception and replace it with an enlightened and compassionate one. In the process, the people have to surrender their own egos and endure material and environmental hardships. December 21, 2012 was identified by the Mayans as the time when this transformation will become most obvious."*

To the Maya the end of their 5,126 year long cycle Mesoamerican Long Count calendar meant:

   a.) The time that ushers in positive transformation.
   b.) The time when the world's energetic power that has controlled and manipulated humanity begins to crumble.
   c.) The time when humanity begins to unleash their limitless potential.

The energetic unlocking of the Epsilon energy seal created the Epsilon strand of God's violet energy Quantum Consciousness. This was the violet energy that produced the energetic breaking of water in God's energetic pregnancy and began the energetic delivery of God's energetic fetus.

43 / AWAKEN THE FORCE

8

The Sixth Energy Seal

With the fifth violet energy strand of God's Quantum Consciousness complete the sixth energy seal was energetically unlocked on the Energetic Blueprint of life.

I saw the sixth energy seal energetically unlock on the Energetic Blueprint of life and was zinged that Quantum Consciousness refers to it as the Zeta seal. It was energetically unlocked on December 21, 2012 at 11:11:12 GMT.

With Zeta unlocked I saw in the inner energetic womb that our Universe began to expand from its tiny position at 9 o'clock to become the entire energetic fetus. I watched as the violet energy of Quantum Consciousness entered the Universe.

I was one with the Quantum Consciousness of God as it entered the Universe racing through the cosmos of time. I remember seeing the Earth move towards us at a lightning speed then suddenly the Quantum Consciousness of God had reached its destination and enveloped every living person.

I was zinged that the Quantum Consciousness of God entered the physical realm at the energetic unlocking of the fifth energy seal. It entered the physical realm to energetically free humanity from its energetic captivity that was put on them by the pale lightning bolt during the energetic unlocking of the fourth energy seal.

The energetic unlocking of the Zeta energy seal created the Zeta strand of God's violet energy Quantum Consciousness. This was the violet energy that began the energetic dilation of God's energetic pregnancy.

9

The Seventh Energy Seal

With the sixth violet energy strand of God's Quantum Consciousness complete the seventh energy seal was energetically unlocked on the Energetic Blueprint of life.

I saw the seventh energy seal energetically unlock on the Energetic Blueprint of life and was zinged that Quantum Consciousness refers to it as the Eta seal. It was energetically unlocked on December 21, 2012 at 11:11:13 GMT.

My next zing from Quantum Consciousness inspired me that the Eta energy strand will be completed on December 21, 2082 at 11:11:12 GMT.

I was zinged that by this time humanity will have made their most important chose in life. Their chose will be to either free themselves from their energetic captivity or remain a slave to their energetic captivity. It will be during this time that the Quantum

Consciousness energetic trigger point will happen. This point will be when 144,000 individuals are energetically sealed as the force of God's Quantum Consciousness.

The energetic unlocking of the Eta energy seal created the Eta strand of God's violet energy Quantum Consciousness. This was the violet energy that continues the energetic dilation of God's energetic pregnancy.

49 / AWAKEN THE FORCE

10

The Eighth Energy Seal

With the seventh violet energy strand of God's Quantum Consciousness complete the eighth energy seal was energetically unlocked on the Energetic Blueprint of life.

I saw the eighth energy seal energetically unlock on the Energetic Blueprint of life and was zinged that Quantum Consciousness refers to it as the Theta seal. It will be energetically unlocked on December 21, 2082 at 11:11:13 GMT. I was zinged that the Theta energy seal will last for 1000 years.

I saw within the inner energetic womb that when the Theta energy seal was unlocked all of God's 100 trillion energetic cells were transfigured from red to violet.

I then saw the upper half of the inner energetic womb become alive. As it came alive it created a 3D circular vortex of light that spiraled in a clockwise direction. I watched as the violet energetic fetus of God began to move towards the circular vortex of light in the upper half of the inner energetic womb.

The energetic unlocking of the Theta energy seal created the Theta strand of God's violet energy Quantum Consciousness. This was the violet energy that will complete the energetic dilation of God's energetic pregnancy.

11

The Ninth Energy Seal

With the eighth violet energy strand of God's Quantum Consciousness complete the ninth energy seal was energetically unlocked on the Energetic Blueprint of life.

I saw the ninth energy seal energetically unlock on the Energetic Blueprint of life and was zinged that Quantum Consciousness refers to it as the Iota seal. It will be energetically unlocked on December 21, 3082 at 11:11:13 GMT.

I then saw the upper half of the inner energetic womb become alive. As it came alive the energetic fetus of God moved further into the 3D circular vortex of light that was spiraling in a clockwise direction. I saw that the head of God's energetic fetus had disappeared into the light of the 3D circular vortex.

The energetic unlocking of the Iota energy seal created the Iota strand of God's violet energy Quantum Consciousness. This was the violet energy that will begin the energetic birth of God's infinite, eternal, energetic body.

55 / AWAKEN THE FORCE

12

The Tenth Energy Seal

With the ninth violet energy strand of God's Quantum Consciousness complete the tenth energy seal was energetically unlocked on the Energetic Blueprint of life.

I saw the tenth energy seal energetically unlock on the Energetic Blueprint of life and was zinged that Quantum Consciousness refers to it as the Omega seal. The time of its unlocking was not revealed to me and is only known by the Quantum Consciousness of God.

I saw in the inner energetic womb that when the energetic unlocking of the Omega energy seal happened the full term violet energy fetus of God disappeared further and further into the light of the 3D vortex until it was completely gone.

The disappearance of the energetic fetus of God into the light of the 3D vortex, which is the sun, overwhelmed me with an unexplainable euphoric emotion of joy.

I then saw within the inner energetic womb a massive explosion similar to what I witnessed at the energetic unlocking of the first energy seal except this time the inner energetic womb went barren just as it had been prior to the energetic unlocking of the first energy seal.

The energetic unlocking of the Omega energy seal created the Omega strand of God's violet energy Quantum Consciousness. This was the violet energy that will complete the energetic birth of God's infinite, energetic eternal body.

The main attraction from my NDE revealed the following cross section and meaning of God's violet energy Quantum Consciousness.

EVOLUTION of ENERGETIC PREGNANCY	TIME	ENERGETIC SEAL	
Energetic Conception	13.75 billion years ago	ALPHA	VIOLET ENERGY
Beginning of Energetic Gestation	+ 1 second	BETA	
Continuance of Energetic Gestation	+ 2 seconds	GAMMA	
Endurance of Energetic Conception	+ 3 seconds	DELTA	
Energetic Breaking of Water	Dec. 21, 2012, 11:11:11 G.M.T	EPSILON	
Beginning of Energetic Dilation	Dec. 21, 2012, 11:11:12 G.M.T	ZETA	
Continuance of Energetic Dilation	Dec. 21, 2012, 11:11:13 G.M.T	ETA	
Completion of Energetic Dilation	Dec. 21, 2082, 11:11:13 G.M.T	THETA	
Beginning of Energetic Pregnancy	Dec. 21, 3082, 11:11:13 G.M.T	IOTA	
Completion of Energetic	TBD	OMEGA	

Part 3

Today's 70 Year Transformation

13

Energy

"I want to know all of God's thoughts all the rest are just details"

Albert Einstein

I was inspired when my soul came back into my body on June 25, 1996 that everything was going to be fine. I remember the doctor stitching my throat up. I remember being wheeled out of the emergency room into my private room at the Bella Coola Hospital when the procedure was completed. However, what I remembered most was how am I ever going to communicate what just happened to me during my NDE.

I couldn't stop feeling and sensing the profundity of what I had just been downloaded with yet I had no idea of where or how to start communicating it. How could I communicate and deliver what just happened to me in a way that would capture the imagination and impact others. I knew I had just been exposed to the meaning and wisdom of the force and Quantum Consciousness of life that our souls know is true, yet I had no idea how to begin communicating it.

As I look back on the 18 years since my soul returned from my NDE I can clearly see I was on my post NDE journey to understand how best to communicate the Quantum Consciousness of God in the most effective way. What impressed me the most about my post NDE journey was that it was a real life extension and continuation of my NDE except I was alive.

Miraculously as Quantum Consciousness's perspective on something was being revealed to me I was able to comprehend it from the perspective of Quantum Consciousness. I know if I had not had my NDE and had not been downloaded with the intel of God's Quantum Consciousness I would not have been able to sense this.

Circumstances would appear in many different ways, through a conversation, a sign on a bus or a radio program, but mostly they came from within in the form of intuitive promptings. It was like I was wearing energetic antennas of Quantum Consciousness and whenever I needed to interpret its meaning and perspective they would be turned on to reveal it.

Another interesting aspect of my post NDE journey was that many would try derailing me from it even though they had no idea I was even on it.

Very early in my post NDE journey I realized that the existence of God is the most polarizing question amongst man today. There are many who sit in the yes camp and believe that God exists and many who sit in the no camp and do not believe that God exists.

The existence of God is something that has never been proven. It's not like anyone has ever been able to say yep, there's God. The more I was inspired about this, the more I was impressed that life has always been trying to solve its most polarizing question about the existence of God without its most important piece of the equation.

The missing piece of the equation regarding the existence of God has been the understanding of energy. What it is, where it comes from, why it exists, how it works and yes where it's going.

During my NDE, I encountered the Quantum Consciousness of God who revealed its infinite wisdom about energy to me. It revealed how energy has kept and will keep life intact on a day by day, second by second bases until its mastermind plan of life is complete.

My post NDE journey revealed that every femtometre (the size of an atomic nucleus) adheres to energy which is the regulator

Quantum Consciousness uses to steer life towards the completion of its mastermind plan of life. My post NDE journey also revealed that in order to capture the imagination of humanity and solve life's most polarizing question, energy needed to be understood from the perspective of Quantum Consciousness.

My post NDE journey was totally different than my NDE because I did not have the direct energetic contact with Quantum Consciousness like I had during my NDE. My connection was indirect rather than direct. I knew that in order to complete my post NDE journey it would have to happen through the distractions of life that are always present. This was something I did not have to deal with during my NDE. It meant I had to compartmentalize when I was being impressed about something from Quantum Consciousness and when I was not. I had to know when my energetic antennas of Quantum Consciousness were being turned on and what they were revealing. I learned very early they would be turned on at anytime of the day. Whenever they were turned on I needed to listen and understand what I was being downloaded with from Quantum Consciousness. They were and still are my living Quantum Consciousness zings.

My post NDE journey revealed that humanity has understood the micro and macro aspects of energy. They are believed to be separate and actually repel each other.

Without their final piece of connectivity, science has identified the micro aspect of energy as the atom and spirituality has identified the macro aspect of energy as God. I was inspired that both appear to be unrelated because they are missing their final piece of connectivity which is energy.

Science's micro aspect of energy and spiritualities macro aspect of energy act like the same poles of a magnet and always repel each other. This is why the existence of God has been life's most polarizing question. Without the connectivity of Quantum Consciousness's perspective on energy they will always repel each other and will always appear to be separate.

Perhaps it was Albert Einstein who understood this best when he said *"Science without religion is lame, religion without science is blind"*

Science began to comprehend its micro aspect of energy 2500 years ago. It was the Greek philosopher Democritus who theorized there is an indivisible state of matter. He named the indivisible state of matter "atomos" meaning not to cut.

Science developed Democritus' theory further when the English chemist John Dalton's (1766-1844) atomic theory postulated all matter was made up of atoms. Dalton's atomic theory quickly became the theoretical foundation of chemistry. Over the last 120 years science has developed Dalton's theory further.

In 1897, Sir Joseph John Thompson (1856-1940) totally changed the atom's perspective by discovering the electron.

In 1911, Ernest Rutherford (1871-1937) discovered the atoms nucleus.

In 1913, Neils Bohr (1885-1962) proposed that electrons orbit the nucleus without losing energy.

In 1932, James Chadwick (1891-1974) identified the neutron, a particle with mass but no charge.

In 1964 physicists Murray Gell-Mann and George Zweig independently proposed the atom's fundamental constituent and elementary particle is the quark.

However, prior to the 1970's, science did not understand how the atom was held together. It was the discovery of the quark that revealed the atom is sub atomically held together by quarks and a strong binding force. Science confirms the atom's subatomic strong binding force is about 100 times stronger than the electromagnetic force and orders of magnitude stronger than gravity. This strong binding force is identified by its red, green and blue colors and gluons. It has no effect outside the atom's nucleus.

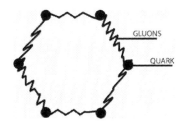

The atoms subatomic structure of strong force and quarks.

Thanks to science, Democritus' 2500 year old theory of the atomos has been proven right down to its energetic 6 quark hexagram and strong binding force red, green and blue energy that holds the atom together.

To understand just how infinitesimal the atom is, a person weighing 70kg is estimated to have 7,000,000,000,000,000,000,000,000,000 atoms in their body and there are an estimated 1 septenvigintillion, 1,000,000,000,000,000,000,000,000,000,000,000,000, 000,000,000,000,000,000,000,000,000,000,000,000 atoms in the Universe.

Archaeologists believe spirituality began some 300,000 years ago at man's first burial sites. The expectation of placing a corpse underground was for the soul of the individual to more easily reach the afterlife. Further, archeological evidence of spiritual faith is seen in late Stone Age (13,000-50,000 years ago) artifacts that represented spiritual ideas. Spirituality's faith is a confidence, trust and hope in some mysterious all powerful 3rd party entity and/or the advancement of humanity towards this unknown all powerful entity. Spirituality identifies this unknown powerful entity as God.

Today, 70% of our global population belongs to 1 of 4 major religions. Christianity has an estimated 2.1 billion followers, Islam has an estimated 1.5 billion followers, Hinduism has an estimated 900 million followers and Buddhism has an estimated 376 million followers. Also, there are thousands of other spiritual faiths that point to an acceptance of God.

I was inspired during my post NDE journey that the best way to describe spirituality is it is an energetic wheel with energetic spokes that all connect to its energetic hub.

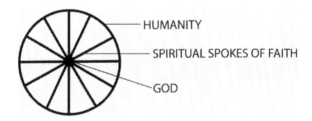

The energetic wheel of spirituality.

The energetic hub of the energetic wheel of spirituality is God and there are many different faiths or beliefs that connect with the energetic hub of God.

Faith is the energetic spokes of the energetic wheel of spirituality. Faith is a confidence, trust and hope that life is moving towards not only improving the state of humanity but also activating itself with God. Buddhism believes an improved state of an individual happens with an awakening or enlightenment. Hinduism believes man is not limited to their body and minds, they further believe the soul is a spark of God. Christianity and Islam take the confidence, trust and hope of faith one step further by describing that this Oneness with God will occur in a paradise or New Heaven/New Earth.

There are two reasons why so many different spokes of faith exist today. The first is to offer humanity as many different options as possible to comprehend and accept that there is a God. Think about it, if there was only one energetic spoke of faith, faith would not have such a mass appeal; it would be dictatorial and autocratic.

The second reason why faith has existed is to stop humanity from annihilating themselves that quite possibly without faith, could already have happened. The spokes of faith have provided humanity with the compassion and empathy to not prematurely eradicate ourselves and to accept that there is a higher power and energy that has created life and is in control of everything.

As long as an energetic spoke of faith connect with the hub of God it does not matter which spoke of faith a person follows or believes in as they are all vitally important to the overall balance of the energetic wheel of spirituality.

My post NDE journey inspired me with the complete perspective of Quantum Consciousness regarding energy. It revealed that the violet 6 point hexagram energy centers and violet energy Quantum Consciousness I encountered during my NDE and the atoms 6 point hexagram quarks and strong force energy are one and the same. Both are the energetic signature of Quantum Consciousness.

The 6 point hexagram creates a compound of two equilateral triangles that produce a star. It is the star that symbolizes the perfect state of balance achieved between humanity and God. It is the energetic foundation of both the micro and macro aspects of energy.

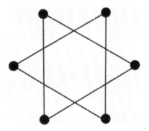

The star symbolizes the perfect state of balance between humanity and God. It is the energetic foundation of both the atom and Quantum Consciousness.

I was further impressed during my post NDE journey that science refers to an energetic conduit of connectivity that connects everything as its superstring theory. Superstrings connect the atoms' Quantum Consciousness with the Quantum Consciousness of God I encountered during my NDE. Superstrings act as energetic telephone lines that energetically communicate the wisdom of the God's Quantum Consciousness with every atom to ensure that God's mastermind plan of life will be completed.

This is how and why the Quantum Consciousness of God regulates life. Energy is the regulator of Quantum Consciousness that is moving life towards completing God's mastermind plan of life and energetic birth of its infinite, eternal energetic body of violet energy Quantum Consciousness.

Up until my June 25, 1996 NDE the Quantum Consciousness of God had only been revealed 4 times in the history of mankind.

14

Transfiguration

"Energy cannot be created or destroyed. It can only be changed from one form to another."

Albert Einstein

I was inspired during my post NDE journey that Quantum Consciousness's perspective of energy had only been revealed 4 times throughout the history of mankind. The purpose of Quantum Consciousness revealing its perspective of energy has always been and always will be about inspiring transformation.

Quantum Consciousness previously revealed its perspective of energy to Jesus, Buddha, Moses and Elijah. Transformation was not the only benefit for Quantum Consciousness to reveal its perspective of energy to the fab 4. The other benefit why Quantum Consciousness revealed its violet energy force to the fab 4 was to reveal its ultimate gift of transfiguration.

Transfiguration is what empowered the fab 4's ascension.

Transfiguration is the energetic potential of humanity. Transfiguration changes our body and mind's subatomic red, green and blue strong binding force energy into the violet energy force of God's Quantum Consciousness. The ascension of Jesus, Buddha, Moses and Elijah was because their atoms had transfigured from their red, green and blue subatomic strong binding force energy into the violet energy force of God's Quantum Consciousness.

It is the violet energy force of God's Quantum Consciousness that transfigures organic compounds into inorganic compounds. This is how the body and minds of Jesus, Buddha, Moses and Elijah were able to ascend as there was no carbon based sub atomic energy in their atoms at the moment of their ascension. Their atoms were sub atomically transfigured from red, green and blue carbon based energy into the violet energy force of Quantum Consciousness.

Quantum Consciousness transcends time and exists in both the physical realm and the spiritual realm. If the body and minds of Jesus, Buddha, Moses and Elijah's subatomic energy had not been transfigured to the violet energy force of Quantum Consciousness their atoms energy would have remained carbon based and their body and minds would not have been able to ascend. Transfiguration is Quantum Consciousness's ultimate gift that creates ascension as experienced by the fab 4.

Organic compounds are carbon based, inorganic compounds are not. Carbon based compounds turn to ash when burned, inorganic compounds do not. If the subatomic energy of Jesus, Buddha, Moses and Elijah's atoms had remained carbon based they would not have been able to ascend through the sun as they did because the sun would have scorched them.

Human beings are made up of three components, a mind, a body and a soul. The mind and body consist of organic red, green and blue sub atomic energy while the soul is inorganic. When I died on June 25, 1996 it was not my red, green and blue energy subatomic atoms from my mind and body that crossed over to the other side it was my soul and violet energy thread of Quantum Consciousness that crossed over.

Our souls are not part of our physical anatomy but they are our energetic anatomy and without them our mind and body's atoms have no power or energy. It is our souls that have provided our body and minds with our red, green and blue sub atomic energy. When our souls leave our body they extinguish our subatomic strong binding force energy from our body and minds atoms and they become instantly energy less and dead.

The soul was first discovered by the Swedish scientist, philosopher and theologian Emanuel Swedenborg (1688-1742) around 1742. His manuscript regarding this finding was not published until 1877. He referred to it as spirituous lymph.

Studies have since determined the soul has mass. In 1907, Dr. Duncan MacDougall, an early 20th century physician from Haverhill, Massachusetts, weighed 6 patients who were in the process of dying from tuberculosis. He discovered within minutes after their death, they had an unexplained average weight loss of 21 grams. MacDougall determined this was the average weight of the soul.

In 1988, a noetic science experiment studied the phenomenon of the soul's weight using more sophisticated tools. They performed experiments on 200 terminally ill patients, using a weighing devise that has a margin of error of less than $1/100,000^{th}$ of an ounce. Their experiments showed that at the death of each of these patients, their weight loss was exactly $1/3000^{th}$ of an ounce.

Our souls are energetic threads of the violet energy force of Quantum Consciousness. They are the energetic perfection and perfect love of Quantum Consciousness. This is why our soul's can comprehend the wisdoms of Quantum Consciousness. Wisdom is our soul's food and sustenance that they require in order to sustain their existence. The frequencies of Quantum Consciousness's violet energy wisdoms vibrate differently than the frequencies of knowledge that our minds comprehend.

Inspiration is an example of a Quantum Consciousness energetic wisdom that our soul comprehends. Inspiration is not comprehended by the mind; to our minds inspiration is irrational and illogical. Our souls are able to comprehend 10 wisdoms from Quantum Consciousness. They are inspiration, love, hope, discernment, instinct, intuition, insight, coincidence, déjà vu and imagination.

The mind deflects 9 of our soul's 10 Quantum Consciousness wisdoms simply because it cannot dial into the energetic frequencies of Quantum Consciousness. The only wisdom that resonates with both our soul and mind is love. Our soul has always been able to comprehend the 10 violet energy wisdoms of Quantum Consciousness because our soul is a violet energy thread of Quantum Consciousness and energetically speaks the same language.

My post NDE journey further inspired me that soul and violet energy threads of Quantum Consciousness fall into 1 of 6 soul age groups. Our soul's age groups are old souls, mature souls, middle aged souls, adolescent souls, infant souls and first time souls.

I was inspired that our soul age groups create a bell curve of soul ages. Old souls make up 2.5 per cent of our population. Mature souls make up 13.5 per cent of our population. Middle aged souls make up 34 per cent of our population. Adolescent souls make up 34 per cent of our population. Infant souls make up 13.5 per cent of our population and first time souls make up the final 2.5 per cent of our population.

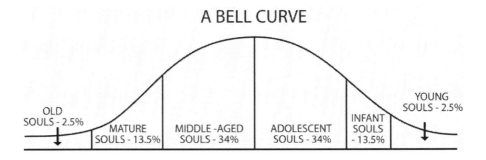

Old souls are those whose soul will be inspired first with the wisdoms of Quantum Consciousness contained in this book. They trust their soul and take greater risks. The more an old soul hears the energetic wisdoms of Quantum Consciousness the more awakened their souls become. Old souls will begin to awaken from their soul's energetic slumber first. It is the old soul who will re-activate and unleash the totality of Quantum Consciousness first. Old souls accept wisdom the fastest because they have crossed out of the physical realm of life into the spiritual realm of life more than any other soul age group. Old souls have a greater soul awareness and are more in tune with the energetic wisdoms of Quantum Consciousness.

Mature souls will be the early adaptors to the wisdoms of Quantum Consciousness. They will not sense their soul's awakening as early as old souls but they will be involved early on in the re-activation and unleashing of the totality of Quantum Consciousness into humanity. Mature souls will accept their soul's awakening because their souls have also crossed out of the physical realm into the spiritual realm many times and can quickly sense the wisdoms of Quantum Consciousness.

The younger the soul is in its physical realm life experiences the less it is able to override the mind. These will be the ones that no matter how hard you work with them regarding Quantum Consciousness it will never sink in because their soul is not ready to awaken and override the energy of their mind. They are the ones who are easy to spot as they are motivated by dollars and cents.

First time souls have no ability to comprehend the existence of their soul and the worst of first time souls manifest their behavior as psychopaths and sociopaths in a selfish and sometimes destructive way on society.

During my post NDE journey I was shown just how easy it is to ascertain the age group of a person's soul. To do so, simply engage a person in meaningful conversation. The more meaningful and deeper that conversation is the older that person's soul is. Always, look intently into a person's eyes and listen to how and what they are saying. The younger the soul is the tougher it will be for them to even make eye contact with you. Also, their verbal responses are only surface chit chat about the weather or some other trivial topic. The deeper the responses of others are means they are more confident because their soul is older.

Always remember that the eyes are the window to the soul. Older souls radiate incredible amounts of light and energy through their eyes and their foreheads tend to energetically glisten and radiate. The oldest of the old souls constantly radiate an energetic light from their eyes much like that of a newborn. Older souls are also able to engage the eyes of others directly in conversation and have surrounded themselves with a strong support system of love.

Old souls are the hungriest to activate their soul again with the violet energy force of Quantum Consciousness to complete their soul's evolution. It is the younger souls who will reject their re-activation and unleashing of the totality of Quantum Consciousness the longest.

15

Changing Your Energetic Disposition

"People will do anything no matter how absurd to stop from facing their souls."

Carl Jung

My next post NDE insight was the discovery of the energetic bridge that we must cross over to unleash the totality of Quantum Consciousness's energetic perfection and perfect love within us. It is our energetic disposition.

Our energetic disposition of who we are is the energetic order of how our body, mind and soul are energetically wired to function as a whole.

Science has done a brilliant job of discovering what our minds and body are and how they work.

Spirituality was the first to realize the existence of the soul and NDE's have confirmed the soul's life pattern. My NDE specifically revealed that every soul is a thread of Quantum Consciousness.

Ever since the first human beings arrived on the planet our energetic disposition has always been wired for survival in the physical realm.

During my post NDE journey I interviewed about 100 people who experienced a near death. Why? To understand what happened to them when their soul left their body during their near death experience.

Amazingly, everyone I interviewed had the same initial experience as their soul left their body at death. Everyone told me when they died; their soul exited their body and hovered above it to review the circumstances of their body's death. Like myself when I died, my soul hovered at the ceiling of the emergency room looking down at my body. Everyone told me that when their soul was satisfied regarding their death it then transitioned out of the physical realm into the spiritual realm.

Most souls were greeted by comforting entities that they were familiar with upon arriving in the spiritual realm, for some it was a long lost relative and friend who had departed. For a few it was

Jesus and one gentleman from Philadelphia told me he was greeted by butterflies.

Approximately 75 per cent of my interviews were with females and 40 per cent of all deaths were by drowning. One of the most profound NDE's I encountered happened to Judy, whom I interviewed by telephone from California several years ago. Judy had been returning home to her farmhouse from grocery shopping on a sunny Saturday afternoon. When Judy got out of her car she saw her husband come out of the front door of their farmhouse frantically yelling and motioning her to come into the house immediately. Judy left her groceries in the trunk of her car and went into the farmhouse. Her husband told her to go into the room immediately to the right of the front door. Her two children were already in the room. They were visibly shaken and extremely emotional. After Judy had entered the room her husband immediately slammed the door shut behind him. At this moment he pulled out a gun and shot Judy. Judy immediately died; her soul left her body and floated to the top of the room. Judy's soul witnessed her husband fatally shoot their two children and then kill himself. Judy's soul then left the farmhouse.

I found in my interviews that everyone had a completely different spiritual realm experience that was very personal to them. However, everyone agreed they did not want to come back into their bodies after they had died. I was inspired in my post NDE journey that the energy on the other side, in the spiritual realm, is the energetic perfection and perfect love of God's violet energy Quantum Consciousness that every soul knows and requires.

There was no fear or negative energy in the spiritual realm only the energetic perfection and perfect love of God's Quantum Consciousness. When mentioning this to those I was interviewing they all agreed that the energetic perfection and perfect love of God was the energy their souls resonated with and desired. All agreed the energy of God does not have any fear or negativity attached to it. It was because of this that no one wanted to return to their bodies after their deaths because everyone wanted to stay exactly where they were in the spiritual realm with the energetic perfection and perfect love of God. We all knew this is the energy our soul craves and the energy that our soul is. However, like me everyone was told they must return. For many that I interviewed the driving force in their lives to this day is to understand, actualize and complete what it was they were downloaded with during their NDE.

My post NDE journey also impressed me that during Quantum Consciousness's 70 year transformation that we are now in, our souls are here in their final life experience. The 70 year transformation began on December 21, 2012 at 11:11:13 GMT with the energetic unlocking of Eta, the seventh energy seal on God's Energetic Blueprint of life. Our soul's final life experience will complete its evolution. To fulfill our soul's evolution we must energetically re-activate and unleash the totality of Quantum Consciousness which is the energetic perfection and perfect love of God to our body and minds atoms.

Up until this life experience human beings have always been wired to perform life with a survivor mode energetic disposition. This survivor mode energetic disposition has always produced an energetic order of mind, body and soul for all life experiences our soul has previously had. The mind has always been our dominant energetic force and has triggered our body's responses and actions while at the same time the mind has denied the existence of the soul. The mind considers the existence of the soul to be illogical and irrational.

Our survivor mode energetic disposition has always forced the soul to have a back seat, passive, limited role in whatever body it previously existed in. Our soul's past, passive limited role has forced it to only express itself through Quantum Consciousness's 10 energetic wisdoms of inspiration, hope, instinct, intuition, discernment, insight, déjà vu, coincidence, love and imagination. This has been the only means the soul has ever known how to communicate with its body and mind. Therefore, humanity's energetic disposition of mind, body and soul has provided us with the energy to survive but not with the energy to unleash our limitless potential and Quantum Consciousness which completes our soul's evolution.

You are not reading this book by accident. Your soul's final life experience is not to have another silent, passive role. It is not to only communicate Quantum Consciousness's 10 wisdoms; it is to unleash its lead, starring role and your limitless potential as the totality of Quantum Consciousness. Your soul's lead starring role will re-activate and unleash the totality of Quantum Consciousness into every one of your body and mind's atoms. However, for this to happen you must first change your energetic disposition from mind, body and soul to soul, body and mind. Your mind can no longer be your lead energy. In order for your soul to complete its evolution and for you to unlessh your limitless potential and Quantum Consciousness, your soul must become your lead energy.

For your soul this means it will not have another passive existence of limitation. The reason for all your souls past live experiences has been to study and learn the energetic subtleties of the mind and body in order to complete its evolution through you in this life experience. This life experience will complete your soul's evolution and integrate all of its past life learning experiences to change your energetic disposition so that your limitless potential and Quantum Consciousness can be unleashed.

In all your souls past life experiences your soul has created gut feelings that have let your past lives know when something was right for them or when to beware of something that was not right for them. This has not changed in this life experience as your soul has always been there to communicate exactly this way from the inside.

What has changed for your soul in this life experience is that the outside help it has been waiting for has arrived to complete its evolution. Your soul's outside help arrived on December 21, 2012 at 11:11:11 GMT when the violet energy force of Quantum Consciousness left the spiritual realm to begin the energetic delivery in its energetic pregnancy. This is the outside support your soul has been waiting for as the totality of Quantum Consciousness is near to help you complete your soul's evolution. It begins by the changing of your energetic disposition.

The Quantum Consciousness of God is its energetic perfection and perfect love of its mastermind plan of life. It communicates as the energetic frequencies your soul can comprehend. They are the frequencies of wisdom. Wisdom is your soul's violet energy directives that cannot be computed by your mind. Conversely, the soul does not resonate with the lower red, green and blue frequencies of facts and knowledge that your mind comprehends. Knowledge is your energetic food of high fat, high sodium, high sugar and high preservatives. Wisdom is your energetic food of great fiber, high quality protein, unsaturated fats and high plant based nutrients.

Quantum Consciousness resonates with your soul to create your gut feelings in order to unleash your Quantum Consciousness limitless potential. This will never harm you or lead you astray. They will complete your soul's evolution and transfigure your body and minds sub atomic energy from red, green and blue to the violet energy of Quantum Consciousness.

The re-activation and unleashing of the totality of Quantum Consciousness within you energetically transfigures your body and mind sub atomic energy into the violet energy of Quantum Consciousness. Your gut feelings are responses that are meant to remove your body and mind from its finite limitations of the physical world into the limitless potential of Quantum Consciousness that completes your soul's evolution.

Your soul is the most powerful component of who you are. Not only does your soul provide the energy for your mind and body's survival. It also has the ability to transfigure your body and mind sub atomic red, green and blue energy into the violet energy of Quantum Consciousness to unleash your limitless potential. To complete its evolution it must override your mind's control and change your energetic disposition from mind, body and soul to soul, body and mind. This is humanity's next leap forward.

This time, your soul knows through its life energy contract that it agreed to before entering the physical realm; that its role for this life experience through you is different than it has ever been for any other life experience it has ever had. Your soul is not here to experience another passive, silent role. It is in you to unleash its starring, lead, active role which will complete its evolution through the unleashing of your limitless potential and Quantum Consciousness. Your soul is anxiously waiting to re-activate itself again with the totality of Quantum Consciousness in the physical realm through you.

In all previous life experiences your soul has activated itself with the totality of Quantum Consciousness in the spiritual realm after the previous body your soul was in died. However, your soul is here in this life experience to re-activate and unleash the totality of Quantum Consciousness of in the physical realm through you to complete its evolution. Your soul has been preparing for the completion of its evolution ever since its first life experience. Your soul eagerly waits to unleash its limitless potential that begins with the changing of your energetic disposition from mind, body and soul to soul, mind and body.

Your soul and violet energy thread of Quantum Consciousness has always been buried deep inside whatever body it previously had. It was also there when energy was unleashed to become the energetic pulse of life to regulate God's mastermind plan of life to its completion. Your soul's mission has always been to complete its evolution which also completes God's mastermind plan of life.

Your soul knows its purpose in this life experience is to complete its evolution through you. Re-activating with the Quantum Consciousness of God in the physical realm is your soul's mission and purpose in this life experience that completes its evolution. Your soul knows its final life experience is the fulfilling of its past life experience lessons. Your transformation into the totality of Quantum Consciousness must begin with the changing of your energetic disposition.

However, your soul's re-activation and unleashing of the totality of Quantum Consciousness in the physical realm cannot happen until your mind is convinced to allow it to happen. This is the greatest gift your mind can ever receive because it eliminates ego. Energetically ego, Edges God Out. To the mind, the existence of God is illogical and irrational which has always been humanity's energetic conundrum.

During my post NDE journey I was impressed that the weak force of nature and Quantum Consciousness's pale force energy which was unleashed at the energetic unlocking of the fourth energy seal 13.75 billion years ago is how a person's energetic disposition changes. As a violet energy thread of Quantum Consciousness your soul is the ultimate force carrier which identifies your minds particles sub atomically that operate at distances of about 0.1% of the diameter of a proton. It will change the energetic disposition of your mind and eliminate ego when reactivated again with the violet energy Quantum Consciousness of God.

If the weak force of nature did not exist, ego could not be eliminated. Your soul's reactivation with Quantum Consciousness creates your ultimate force carrier that changes the atoms of your mind sub atomically into entirely new elements. It eliminates ego and changes your energetic disposition to unleash your souls lead, starring active role in this life experience through you to complete its evolution.

In order for the mind to eliminate ego and grant the soul the opportunity to complete its evolution it's only fair that your mind comprehends what the soul is, what it has done and what it is doing. Your soul is a violet energy thread of Quantum Consciousness. Its energetic anatomy consists of two parts, an energetic body and an energetic mind. The soul's energetic mind is its collective unconsciousness and the remainder of the soul is its energetic body.

After conception, the initial task of the soul's collective unconsciousness created your brainstem and brain. Your soul's collective unconsciousness also created your energetic traits for this life experience. Your energetic traits are your security, sexuality, identity and spirituality needs.

The body of your soul runs through your spinal cords central canal. It is the soul that carried your energetic blueprint and instructions on how to create you physically — exactly as you are. It did so by creating you from the inside out. The first thing your soul did after conception was protect itself by creating the central canal and the spinal cord. Your soul was given energetic instructions as to how your body and mind was to be created in order that you could be birthed into the physical world exactly as you were.

The central canal of the spinal cord runs longitudinally through the length of your entire spinal cord. It is filled with cerebrospinal fluid. CSF was the first cells created by your soul and collective unconsciousness. CSF is a clear colorless bodily fluid whose main purpose is to create a natural buoyancy for your brain. It allows your brain to not be impaired by its own weight that would choke off your blood supply and immediately kill you. It also protects your brain tissue from injury and provides a chemical stability to your brain. The central canal occludes (closes off) as you age. As you age, your soul and collective unconsciousness reaches its predetermined expiry date for your life experience. At death because your central canal closes off it forces your soul and collective unconsciousness out of the body. This cannot happen when your body and mind's atoms are sub atomically transfigured from their temporary red, green and blue subatomic energy to the violet energy of Quantum Consciousness because your energetic disposition is changed from mind, body soul to soul, body mind.

Central Canal of Spinal Cord

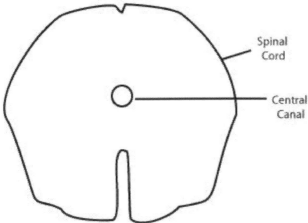

Energetically our minds are made up of 3 energetic aspects, our consciousness, our sub consciousness and our unconsciousness. Within our unconsciousness is our collective unconsciousness which is the essence of our mind. The collective unconsciousness has a dual role as it is part of our minds physical anatomy and it is part of our soul's energetic anatomy.

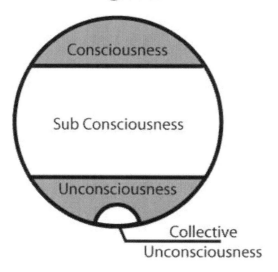

Consciousness is our mind's energetic storage facility that receives and transmits energetic signals. Our consciousness receives energetic signals from one of two directions, either externally from our external stimuli or internally from our subconscious, unconsciousness, collective unconsciousness and soul.

Energy - Thoughts - Actions:

The energy from our external stimuli produces our brain waves. Brain waves are measured by electroencephalography (EEG). EEG records electrical activity along the scalp. It measures voltage fluctuations, which result from ionic current flows within the neurons of the brain.

EEG Recording of Scalp's Electrical Activity

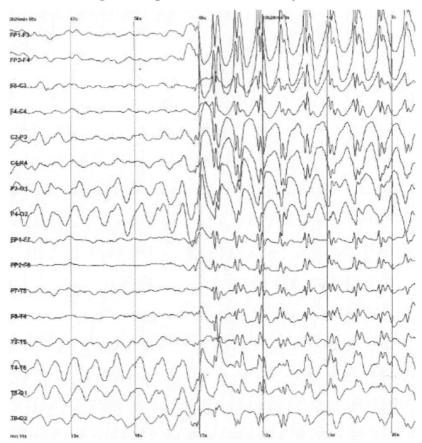

Left-brained dominance indicates a person resonates more with their outer consciousness and external stimuli.

Right-brained dominance indicates a person resonates more with their deeper consciousness and internal stimuli.

Left and Right Brain Thinking:

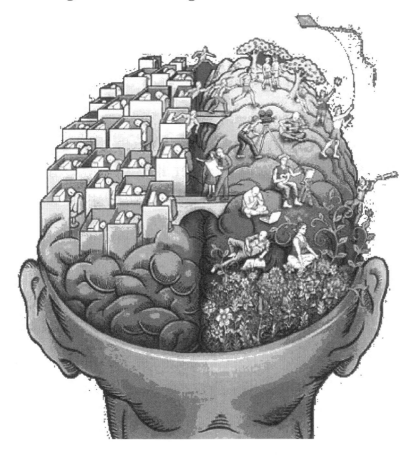

Left-brained people are rational. They respond well to verbal instructions. They use logic to solve problems. They look at things sequentially. They measure differences. They are planned, structured and organized. They prefer established proven information. They prefer multiple-choice questions. They control their feelings. They prefer ranked authority structures. They draw on previously accumulated, organized information. They prefer indoor activities. They are detail oriented - facts rule oriented.

They are also present and past oriented. They prefer the safe course of action. Their soul age makes up the younger ages of the soul age bell curve.

Left-brained people assume vocations such as computer programmers, technicians, engineers, stockbrokers, scientists, accountants, bookkeepers, human resource directors, administrative assistants, lawyers, doctors, bankers and anything to do with finance.

In contrast, right-brained people are intuitive. They solve problems using their intuition and hunches. They respond to demonstrated instructions. They look for patterns and configurations. They look for similarities, are fluid and spontaneous. They prefer elusive, uncertain information and open-ended questions. They prefer drawing. They are free spirits and prefer outdoor activities. Right-brainers use feelings in their decision-making. They are focused on the 'big picture.' They are present and future oriented. They prefer philosophy, religion and spiritual issues. They are impetuous action takers and risk takers. Their soul age makes up the older ages of the soul age bell curve.

Right-brained people assume vocations which involve working with people such as counseling and psychology, where they help solve problems. They are artists, musicians, authors, recreational directors and marketing experts. They hold most of the jobs in retail that deal with other people. They are interior designers, hospitality, hotel workers and sales professionals.

As your soul reverses the energetic disposition of who you are from mind, body, soul to soul, body and mind, your mind begins to move out of its limited consciousness into its sub consciousness, unconsciousness and collective unconsciousness.

In your limited consciousness state the mind accesses at most 10 per cent of its potential. As a result it tends to over think and makes decisions of lower quality. This is the primary reason why teachers tell students to go with their first instinct. The more time spent thinking about the answer the greater the probability it is wrong. Unleashing your minds limitless potential not only extinguishes your ego it also helps to reduce wrong decisions. As your mind goes deeper and moves out of consciousness the better your life's decisions become.

First time souls tend to live in the outer regions of their consciousness and cannot comprehend anything beyond their short term satisfactions from external stimuli. On the other hand, older souls tend to live in the deeper recesses of their consciousness closer to their sub consciousness, unconsciousness and collective unconsciousness and their internal stimuli. It is for this reason that older souls are able to rely more on their soul's promptings.

Changing your energetic disposition is your soul's energetic prerequisite that begins to move it towards completing its evolution.

16

The Illusion

"Reality is merely an illusion, albeit a very persistent one."

Albert Einstein

Changing your energetic disposition and eliminating ego is something your mind does not want to do. However, once your mind understands how it has been manipulated by the prevailing energies of the day that were allowed to enter the Universe at the energetic unlocking of the fourth energy seal, its dominance and control will begin to weaken.

Morpheus referred to it to Neo in the movie, The Matrix, "It is everywhere; it is all around us. Even now, in this very room, you can see it when you look out your window, or turn on your television set. You can feel it when you go to work, when you go to church, when you pay taxes. It is the world that has been pulled over your eyes to blind you from the truth."

What Morpheus was referring to was the energy from the illusion of life that our minds perceive as reality.

The illusion was created by the illusionist. The illusionist has created limitless wealth and power by keeping our minds trapped in his energetic mind prison. His illusion keeps our minds trapped in his energetic mind prison by temporarily providing the fix to our mind's fears and insecurities. The illusionist controls our minds through our addiction to money which satisfies our ego. The secret why the illusionist can keep our minds trapped in his energetic mind prison is money temporarily satisfies our mind's fears and insecurities.

Everything in the world today, including our minds, is controlled by the illusionist and money because it is logical to our minds. The changing of our energetic disposition to soul, body and mind nullifies the illusionist's control over our mind and moves life one step closer to completing God's mastermind plan of life.

Today, we cling to our excess debris like never before. We have become a civilization of hoarders because of our addiction to excess. In 1960, North America had no storage facilities. Today, in North America alone, it is estimated there is over thirty billion cubic feet of storage space. It is leased out to hold the excesses of our debris that our minds cannot consciously rid themselves of, even though most of us no longer use or need it.

The illusionist knows he can easily keep our minds trapped in his energetic mind prison because of our mind's need of excess. Excess is our short term crutch that temporarily eliminates our mind's fears and insecurities and satisfies our ego. The illusionist has created numerous fear and insecurity tricks to keep our minds trapped in his energetic mind prison.

The illusionist's tricks always produce stress. The more fearful and insecure we are, the more stressed we become. The more stressed we become the more destructive we are and the greater toll it takes on our mental, emotional, physical and spiritual well being. Our minds have been conditioned to believe that our short term fix of money is all they need.

The illusionist's drug of money temporarily soothes our mind's fears and insecurities by satisfying our ego. The mind is constantly being bombarded with something that will satisfy our ego and short term needs. Our energetic reality is the more we have, the more we crave and the more we don't have, the more we want. Our minds are absolutely addicted to money and like any addict our mind requires more of it to satisfy its ongoing addiction. Money is the illusionist's drug which keeps his illusion alive and keeps our minds energetically trapped in his energetic mind prison.

The illusionist has made the energy of money life's dominant force because of our addiction to it. The illusionist's energetic mind prison has spun its illusionary energetic web over our mind to blind us from understanding its true intent.

The History of Money

Before money, people bartered. The system of barter was an exchange of goods or services for other goods or services, (e.g., a bag of rice for a bag of beans). However, carrying bags of rice, beans or other commodities became difficult as they would become perishable and difficult to store.

The Barter System

In 700 BC, coins began to appear in the Western world as an exchange to buy and sell. Some of the earliest known paper money dates back to China, where its issuance became common around the year 960.

Approximately 250 years ago, the illusionist figured out how to control money. He placed his assets in financial instruments and circulated them through the world as stocks, bonds and debt which made it impossible to find out the truth regarding the illusionist and his illusion.

The illusionist creates and controls his social contract of money which gives him his power. He has made money the matrix to everything that is both feared and loved at the same time. Money is loved because it produces the roof over our heads and sustenance to survive. Money is feared because of the stress and destruction it creates. Money is what drives the world's economies and builds our consciousness's self worth. A lack of it produces fears and insecurities that lead to stress. The game of the illusionist has been brilliantly crafted and purposely hidden from your mind.

Understanding today's illusion is something the illusionist DOES NOT want your mind to understand because it begins to unravel his illusion and unlock the door of his energetic mind prison where your mind presently resides. The unlocking of your energetic mind prison door begins with the realization that money is only a commodity, an item of trade or commerce.

Every commodity has a manufacturing and distribution cycle which operates in the following manner:

First, the commodity is produced by the manufacturer. Next, the manufacturer sells their finished commodity to their manufacturing rep, for a profit. The manufacturing rep is responsible for distributing the commodity within a large geographical region, such as a country. To effectively distribute the manufactured commodity within its geographical region, the manufacturing rep resells it to a retailer, for a profit. The retailer makes the final sale of the commodity to the consumer, for yet another profit.

Lumber is an example of a commodity. The manufacturing and distribution cycle of lumber is as follows:

Step #1 - Trees are cut down and manufactured by a lumber manufacturer in order to produce the finished commodity of lumber.

Step #2 - The lumber manufacturer sells his finished product to his manufacturing rep to distribute it within a large geographical region.

Step #3 – The manufacturing rep resells the lumber to his retailers in smaller geographical areas to sell locally.

Step #4 – The retailer completes the final sale of lumber to the consumer.

What the illusionist has kept hidden from you is money also follows the same manufacturing and distribution cycle as lumber and every other commodity. However, with money, the illusionist has added extra controlling features to his commodity of money which other commodities do not have. It is through the revealing of this information that your mind can begin to free itself from the illusionist's energetic mind prison as the illusionist's matrix begins to unravel in your mind.

The manufacturing and distribution cycle of money is as follows:

Step #1 - Money is manufactured by its manufacturer. The manufacturing of money is completed by central banks the illusionist owns. The Bank of International Settlements in Basel, Switzerland is the central bank of central banks. It controls all other central banks. Central banks are banking cartels with monolithic powers to create a nation's money supply. The United States central bank is the Federal Reserve.

"The Federal Reserve is an independent agency and there is no other agency of government which can overrule any actions that we take."

Allan Greenspan

Unlike lumber and every other manufactured commodity, there are NO hard costs to the manufacturing of money. Money manufacturers do not need to cut down trees like lumber manufacturers. They do not need to extract precious metals from the ground like a precious metal manufacturer does. Money is manufactured out of thin air with only a nominal printing cost associated with it.

Step #2 - The illusionist creates money from thin air through central banks. Unlike other commodities, which sell their commodity to their manufacturing reps for a profit, the illusionist, through his central banks, has no costs and everything he does with money is pure profit. To maximize his profit he lends his commodity of money to his manufacturing reps who are the federal governments in the countries where he prints his money. By lending his commodity of money to federal governments, the illusionist still maintains ownership of it and everything that it has created are its collateral until it is paid back in full. Experts have calculated the world's global net worth to be USD -$57 Trillion based on total global assets estimated of USD $223 Trillion and an estimated total global debt of USD $280 Trillion.

Federal governments distribute the illusionist borrowed money within the jurisdiction in which money is printed. There are central banks located in the following countries: Afghanistan, Albania, Algeria, Angola, Argentina, Armenia, Aruba, Australia, Austria, Azerbaijan, Bahamas, Bahrain, Bangladesh, Barbados, Belarus, Belgium, Belize, Benin, Bermuda, Bhutan, Bolivia, Bosnia and Herzegovina, Botswana, Brazil, Burkina Faso, Burundi, Cambodia, Cameroon, Canada, Cape Verde, Cayman Islands, Central African Republic, Chad, Chile, China, Colombia, Congo, The Democratic Republic of the Congo, Costa Rica, Croatia, Cuba, Curaçao, Cyprus, Czech Republic, Denmark, Dominican Republic, Ecuador, Egypt, El Salvador, EQuatorial Guinea, Estonia, Ethiopia,

European Union, Fiji, Finland, France, Gabon, Gambia, Georgia, Germany, Greece, Guatemala, Guinea, Guinea-Bissau, Guyana, Haiti, Honduras, Hong Kong, Hungary, Iceland, India, Indonesia, Iran, Iraq, Ireland, Israel, Italy, Jamaica, Japan, Jordan, Kazakhstan. Kenya, Korea, Kosovo, Kuwait, Kyrgyzstan, Lao, Latvia, Lebanon, Lesotho, Liberia, Libya, Lithuania, Luxembourg, Macao, Macedonia, Madagascar, Malawi, Malaysia, Mali, Malta, Mauritius, Mexico, Moldova, Mongolia, Montenegro, Morocco, Mozambique, Myanmar, Namibia, Nepal, Netherlands, New Zealand, Nicaragua, Niger, Nigeria, Norway, Oman, Organization of Eastern Caribbean States, Pakistan, Papua New Guinea, Paraguay, Peru, Philippines, Poland, Portugal, Qatar, Romania, Russian Federation, Rwanda, Samoa, San Marino, Saudi Arabia, Senegal, Serbia, Seychelles, Sierra Leone, Singapore, Slovakia, Slovenia, Solomon Islands, South Africa, Spain, Sri Lanka, Sudan, Suriname, Swaziland, Sweden, Switzerland, Syrian Arab Republic, Tajikistan, Tanzania, Thailand, Togo, Tonga, Trinidad and Tobago, Tunisia, Turkey, Turkmenistan, Uganda, Ukraine, United Arab Emirates, United Kingdom, United States, Uruguay, Uzbekistan, Vanuatu, Venezuela, Vietnam, Yemen, Zambia and Zimbabwe.

Borrowing means to receive something temporarily from its owner who's expecting it back. Money is all borrowed by the governments of the world who are in huge debt to the central bankers who have lent it to them. Governments collateral to the central bankers for their debt they are owed are the assets within the country. Therefore, because of a governments debt the reality of money and the assets it creates is it's not yours; it never was and never will be. Money and everything that money has created is the central banker's collateral for your government's debt until it is paid off. The illusionist has lulled us into a false sense of security that we own whatever his borrowed drug of money has produced. Even though it may be in your bank account or it may be in assets you own, the ultimate owner of everything is the illusionist and the central banks because of the debt they are owed.

In the illusion, your mind has been tricked to believe that you own money. However, it's not yours, it never was and it never will be. This was evidenced in March 2013 in Cyprus where the biggest bank heist of all time occurred. Bank depositors in Cyprus had 6 billion Euros stolen from their bank accounts overnight to pay back money owed to the central bankers. This led Jeroen Dijsselbloem, the Dutch head of Eurozone finance ministers to boast this would be the model for future bailouts. Beware as the illusionist through his central bankers has revealed his plans of how to take back money that you think is yours and the Cyprus heist shows how easy it is for the illusionist to do. The Cyprus heist was the illusionist dry run to gauge what humanity's reaction would be when money vanishes. Beware, Cyprus was only the beginning.

We are all merely money junkies who have been taught to hoard our fix and try to make sure we never run out of it.

One way to counter this would be to go on the offensive and get all of a bank's account holders together and storm the bank and have every account holder demand their money back in cash. First, no bank would ever be able to handle such a request because at best a bank's cash reserves are only a fraction of their cash deposits. Second, a demand of this magnitude would force the central bankers to either print enough cash to handle this demand or create mass hysteria because the illusion of money would be revealed.

From his position of power and as the owner of money, the illusionist calls the shots in the illusion. He controls all governments by financing them. He has perfected his control over all governments because governments require money in order to survive. The illusionist always stays behind the scenes, but pulls the strings for everything your consciousness perceives as reality. He controls the media, the governments, the central intelligence agencies, the banks, the stock markets and virtually every other aspect of your horizontal, linear, measured reality. This allows him to control everything in his energetic illusion including your mind through your addiction to money.

"Some of the biggest men in the United States are afraid of something. They know there is a power somewhere, so organised, so subtle, so watchful, so interlocked, so complete, so pervasive that they had better not speak above their breath when they speak in condemnation of it."

President Woodrow Wilson

Step #3 - Lending money to governments is how the illusionist holds absolute power over all nations and humanity. The illusionist knows he is safe because governments control the people in their country through law enforcement agencies and ultimately the military if the people become restless.

One of the games of the illusion has been capitalism. The business of the capitalist in the illusion has been the management of capital. Governments lend the illusionist borrowed money to their retailers, who are the banks and brokerage houses within the geographical jurisdiction that money is printed in. The key individuals within capitalism are known as the enlightened ones because of their inside positions within the illusion.

The Latin word for the enlightened ones who have the inside position in the game of capitalism is illuminatus or illuminati. It should not be surprising the enlightened ones occupy the top rungs of the capitalist wealth and power ladder. Their official title is investment banker.

"Who controls the money can control the world."

Henry Kissinger

"It is well enough that people of the nation do not understand our banking and monetary system, for if they did, I believe there would be a revolution before tomorrow morning."

Henry Ford

The insiders of capitalism are mobile; they do not get tied to any given location. Capital is very fluid and liquid. It flows to where growth is realized the fastest. We see this today with the countless number of ghost towns that exist globally. These towns are now rusting away because capital has vacated them, only to realize faster growth elsewhere.

Another popular game played by the illusionist creates profits through war. The illusionist finances both sides of most military conflicts. This can be seen over the last 100 years beginning with World War I. Recently the illusionist has discovered how to ratchet war up to its highest stakes by pitting faith and spirituality against each other. Wars of spirituality and faith are his ultimate type of war because now the personal emotion of faith has been brought into the equation of war. These types of wars will never end. This is exactly what the illusionist wants. To the illusionist, war is his casino and the gamblers in his casino battle long and hard to borrow more chips of money from him to finance the war. The illusionist decides who will be the victor and the last man standing in all wars.

Wars are always the most profitable game of the illusionist because he also gets to manage the aftermath and reconstruction whenever a war is completed. In wars, millions of people die and while the world mourns, the illusionist already has his post-war reconstruction investments in place to maximise his profits.

It became inevitable that the law of diminishing returns would someday overthrow capitalism. The decline of capitalism began around 1970. This was when capitalism was forced to create greater returns in another way because of relatively flat production levels and consumption. Capitalism began to move production to low income areas of the world in order to produce greater profit margins. As a result, capitalism had 4 decades of artificial growth. The end of capitalism was in September of 2008, with the financial collapse that brought the global financial system to its knees.

The illusionist thinks and plans his game of control through the illusion many decades in advance. To the illusionist, the illusion is like a game of chess and he owns and controls all the pieces on the chess board including the minds of humanity. He decides how much money to print and he only prints as much as he needs in order to use it as he sees fit to bring about his end goal. The illusionist is our real-life Monopoly banker. He prepares and plans new games thirty to fifty years in advance. Capitalism was handy, but it ran its course in 2008, as he planned for it to do. The illusionist brought capitalism to its knees by a controlled demolition of real estate bubbles and toxic derivatives.

Like any great creator, the illusionist creates from the back end knowing what he wants to accomplish, and then fills in the details in order to make it work. Post-capitalism was created this same way. Post capitalism can be traced back to 1980 in the US and the UK. In Europe the Maastricht treaty led to the creation of the Euro. The new game began to reveal itself with privatisation, free trade agreements and the establishment of the regulation busting World Trade Organization, as the illusionist prepared his New World Order and next game of globalization.

Since 2008, globalization has accelerated rapidly. The new regime of global government is being established in order to replace the existing forms of government. This can be seen with the creation of the World Trade Organization, the International Monetary Fund and the World Bank. Globalization or new world order has already begun to carve the world into super states. The European Union and African Union are already a reality, while the North American Union of Canada, United States and Mexico will soon become a reality, along with Asia's Pacific Union.

Globalization has already started within the corporate world. In the United States the number of corporations controlling the U.S. Media has amalgamated from 50 to 5 since 1983. Get ready for the marching orders of globalization as they come directly from the illusionist through the central bank of central banks.

The game of globalization is much easier for the illusionist to control. There are fewer pieces in his illusions chess game to manage. Instead of dealing with all of the various countries' governments, it will become centralised and easier to run. The illusionist is restructuring and downsizing his machine in order to maximise his profits. He is currently preparing to downsize his machine by shedding himself of the expense created by countless governments. To the illusionist, globalization is the downsizing and restructuring of his world corporation. It would appear to be a brilliant scheme, if you're the illusionist and within his tight knit group of enlightened ones. However, less than .0001% of humanity is part of his clique.

The illusionist began globalization slowly. Over the last forty years he tried it out by introducing policies and practices in third world countries where the resistance would be minimal. However, he has now begun to transition these policies to first world countries. As in all third world countries, mass poverty and police state tyranny is right around the corner for those living in first world countries.

The anti-globalist movement began resisting globalization. It started near the end of the 20th century as more and more people began to understand what globalization really meant. This concerned the illusionist. How dare his slaves blindly not accept what he was doing as we have always done in the past.

In November of 1999, the illusionist tipped his hand by authorizing a police state tyranny response against the resistance to globalization in Seattle, Washington. This included incapacitating people by holding their eyes open and pepper spraying them. The Seattle police response actually helped strengthen the anti-globalization movement, as globally, more and more people began to see the illusionist's next game and didn't like it. This peaked in Genoa, Italy, in July of 2001, when violence from both sides resembled a war.

The illusionist knew humanity's growing resistance to globalization had to change. This change became a reality on September 11, 2001 as on this fateful day globalization went underground and disappeared from our public consciousness. Suddenly, the illusionist had shifted our attention away from globalization, toward a whole new enemy. New wars were started as the illusionist began his most profitable game of war all over again.

Globalization ushers in the illusionist's new game, in this post-capitalism era. The one world system is fast approaching. The illusionist has created his new global culture and control mechanisms of poverty and regimentation. This controls those who live in first world countries similar to what has happened to those who live in third world countries. The only thing standing in the way of the successful implementation of the illusionist's end goals is the transforming of God's violet energy Quantum Consciousness of energetic perfection and perfect love in humanity and in money. This has never been more needed than it is today.

Step #4 - Money retailers make their final sale of money to consumers, adding yet another premium to it. Banks sell money to the public at prime +. Initially, less risky ventures were charged a lower interest rate, while riskier ventures were charged a higher interest rate. The illusionist has even allowed banks to create their own mini illusion by the issuance of credit to consumers. By giving you a false sense of security through credit the illusionist has kept your mind from knowing his true intentions and larger plans he has in store for you.

With the exception of money, this is where a commodity's manufacturing and distribution cycle ends – not so for the illusionist. He has added two additional control mechanisms against you to get back as much of his manufactured commodity of money as possible.

To satisfy the illusionist's massive insecurities and fear regarding his illusion being exposed he needed to place more control over you. He has done so with two added monetary control mechanisms.

Illusionist Control Mechanism #1 is about taking back from you as much of his manufactured commodity of money as possible. This control mechanism is similar to a computer manufacturer legally stealing back one-half of a computer you just bought from him.

This is what the illusionist does with money. The illusionist accomplishes this with taxes, fees and levies through his wholesale distributor of governments. Taxes will never stop being levied; they will only continue to increase with more new taxes, fees and levies being instituted to take away as much money from you as possible. This is an absolute guarantee.

In many countries around the world taxes were introduced as a temporary means to fund World War I. Here is a partial list of some of today's taxes and fees levied by governments: accounts receivable tax, airline surcharge tax, airline fuel tax, airport maintenance tax, building permit tax, cigarette tax, corporate income tax, death tax, dog license tax, driving permit tax, environmental tax, excise tax, federal income tax, federal unemployment tax, fishing license tax, food license tax, gasoline tax, goods and services tax, gross receipts tax, harmonized sales tax, hunting license tax, hydro tax, inheritance tax, interest tax, liquor tax, luxury taxes, marriage license tax, Medicare tax, mortgage tax, personal income tax, property tax, prescription drug tax, provincial income tax, provincial sales tax, real estate tax, recreational vehicle tax, retail sales tax, service charge tax, school tax, federal, provincial and municipal telephone surcharge taxes, telephone minimum usage surcharge tax, vehicle license registration tax, vehicle sales tax, water tax, watercraft registration tax, well permit tax and workers compensation tax.

I am sure there are more government taxes, fees and levies I have missed, but you get the picture. The illusionist has made sure a tax structure is enforced in all countries in order to take back from you as much of his manufactured commodity of money as possible.

This satisfies his massive fears and insecurities and limits you so that his game is not exposed. It also keeps your mind locked away in his energetic mind prison, addicted and needing your next fix of his money.

Illusionist Control Mechanism #2 is again about legally stealing back as much of his social contract of money as possible. This is similar to a computer manufacturer charging you a user fee to store your half a computer within his storage facility. This is what banks do with money. They charge you transaction fees on everything you do in their bank for the privilege of keeping your after-tax money with them.

In the first quarter of 2010, the total profits of Canada's 6 biggest banks surged to $5.3 Billion dollars. The first quarter profit of the Bank of Nova Scotia was $988 million, the Canadian Imperial Bank of Commerce's profit was $652 million, the Bank of Montreal's profit was $657 million, National Bank's profit was $215 million, the Royal Bank's profit was $1.5 billion and TD Canada Trust profit was $1.29 billion. Ironically, some of this profit was a result of the fees banks charged you for the privilege of holding your money.

"The obsession for maximizing profits to shareholders has got to be seen as abusive, as dangerous and as one of the most appalling situations on this planet because it makes for criminal behavior."

Anita Roddick, Founder of The Body Shop

The illusion will not change. It does not matter which political party is in control of a country's federal government as the outcome will always be what the illusionist dictates. The illusionist's plan is simple; it is to keep your mind and as many minds as possible trapped in his energetic mind prison through our addiction to his social contract of money.

The gross world product (GWP) is the combined gross national product of every country in the world. GWP is the balance between global imports and exports. In 2012 the GWP totaled US$84.97 trillion. This produced a per person GWP capita of approximately US$11,800 per person. US$84.97 trillion or US$11,800 is what the Illusionist needed to create through his central banks in 2012 to keep his game alive.

The illusionist has no reason to let your mind out of his energetic mind prison. In fact, the more you are addicted to his drug of money the easier it is for him to keep your mind locked up in his energetic mind prison.

The Dalai Lama described humanity's involvement in the illusion this way "he sacrifices his health in order to make money. Then he sacrifices money to replicate his health. And then he is so anxious about the future that he does not enjoy the present; the result being that he does not live in the present or the future; he lives as if he is never going to die, and then dies having never really lived."

17

Activations of Transformation

"We shall require a substantially new way of thinking if mankind is to survive."

Albert Einstein

By this point in the book many of you will be awakening with gut feelings of excitement, inspiration and hope. Some may be awakening to the feelings of shock and anger because of what the illusion has kept hidden from your mind. Whatever your gut feelings may be, they are the energetic moment your soul has been waiting to create. This is the awakening of your soul and is the required first step that will allow your mind to escape from the energetic mind prison it is trapped in.

If you're not here yet certainly you will be by the end of this chapter. Your soul is about to awaken to the violet energy

Quantum Consciousness of God that as of December 21, 2012 is now in the physical realm.

The Quantum Consciousness of God is in the physical realm to reactivate itself with your soul like it has always done in the spiritual realm. For the first time ever your soul will not need to experience a death or a near death, as it always has had to experience in its past lives to re-activate itself with Quantum Consciousness.

Your soul has always re-activated itself with Quantum Consciousness in the spiritual realm whenever the previous body it resided in either died or had a NDE such as I had on June 25, 1996. This re-activation process of your soul with Quantum Consciousness does not change.

However, this time your soul knows its re activation with Quantum Consciousness is to be in the physical realm and not the spiritual realm. As a violet energy thread of Quantum Consciousness your soul knows that Epsilon, the fifth energy seal was energetically unlocked on God's Energetic Blueprint of life on December 21, 2012 at 11:11:11 GMT. Your soul knows that because of the energetic unlocking of the Epsilon seal the totality of Quantum Consciousness's violet energy has entered the physical realm. Your soul knows that in this life experience through you it will reactivate itself with the violet energy totality of Quantum

Consciousness in the physical realm. This is why your soul came back and created you.

I was inspired during my post NDE journey that our soul's reactivation with Quantum Consciousness in the physical realm is through activations of transformation. Activations of transformation are your soul's energetic mode of connecting with the violet energy force of Quantum Consciousness in the physical realm.

Activations of transformation are your soul's energetic procedure that releases them from their passive silent role and unleashes their lead starring role. They are your soul's development step that will fortify and strengthen your energetic disposition as soul, body and mind so that your limitless potential and Quantum Consciousness can be unleashed.

For your soul this step has been completed numerous times, except this time its host, or you, remains alive. Activations of transformation re-activate the totality of Quantum Consciousness with your soul so that its energetic perfection and perfect love is no longer separated from your soul.

Activations of transformation are the procedure and energetic catalyst that lead to the completion of your soul's evolution. Your soul has gone through all of its life experiences in order to prepare itself for this, its pinnacle life experience so that its evolution can be completed. Your soul's reactivation with Quantum Consciousness transforms your soul from being an unattached single violet energy thread of Quantum Consciousness into the energetic totality and absolute force of Quantum Consciousness's violet energy. Your soul will be re-activated and turned on to become the totality of Quantum Consciousness's power and energy again.

Activations of transformation are the required first step to reactivate the totality of Quantum Consciousness with your soul so that every atom of your being can be transfigured into the violet energy of Quantum Consciousness. Activations of transformation begin your transformation into the totality of Quantum Consciousness and unleash your limitless potential.

Up until now it has only been the fab 4 of Jesus, Buddha, Moses and Elijah that have ever been transformed into the violet energy force of Quantum Consciousness in the physical realm to unleash their limitless potential.

Many have told me that the completion of their activations of transformation was the best thing they have ever done. I have had the privilege to lead many through their activations of transformation to reactivate their soul with the totality of Quantum Consciousness. Activations of transformation are always completed at your leisure in your private domain over telephone or Skype.

To begin your activations of transformation your mind must be slowed down to its Theta brainwave rhythm speed. Your Theta brainwave rhythm speed operates at 4 to 8 cycles per second. This is the brainwave rhythm speed your collective unconsciousness and soul discerns the Quantum Consciousness of God at. It is only your Theta brainwave rhythm speed that can discern your soul's journey and reactivation with God's violet energy Quantum Consciousness.

Activations of transformation are guided out of body experiences for your soul. They produce the same results for your soul as when the body they were previously in died or had a near death and transitioned to the spiritual realm to reactivate with the Quantum Consciousness of God. Your activations of transformation access the deepest recesses of your mind which is your collective unconsciousness. Activations of transformation also access your energetic communication between Quantum Consciousness and your soul.

Your Theta brainwave rhythm speed is your energetic channel that dials in the energetic communication between Quantum Consciousness and your soul. They are the frequencies that your soul and Quantum Consciousness communicate at. It is only through your Theta brainwave rhythm speed that you can discern your soul's reactivation with Quantum Consciousness. It will produce a definite and indisputable impression on you. It is like nothing you have ever experienced before; it will take your mind into hidden energetic dimensions it has previously not known.

Your Theta brainwave speed is different from your Beta brainwave rhythm speed. Your Beta brainwave speed is your mind's brainwave rhythm speed at which your mind through your consciousness comprehends daily life at. It operates at 14 to 39 cycles per second. This speed cannot comprehend the communication of Quantum Consciousness.

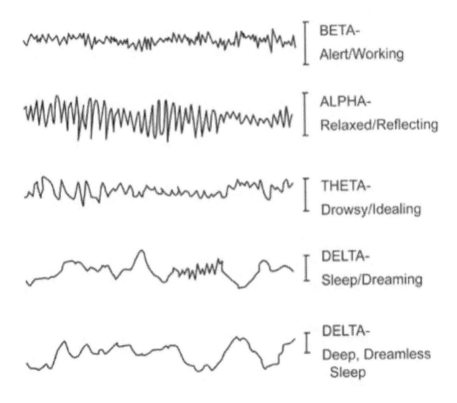

Brainwave Speeds

      1. Beta- 14-39 cycles per second

      2. Alpha- 8-14 cycles per second

      3. Theta- 4-8 cycles per second

      4. Delta- 0-4 cycles per second

Some of the benefits others have told me their activations of transformation have produced are:

1. Develop a greatest awareness of reality,

2. Confirm their immortality,

3. Unleash their limitless potential,

4. Unleash the perfect love, ultra positivity and limitless potential of Quantum Consciousness within them,

5. Unleash the totality of Quantum Consciousness into their life,

6. Escape from the illusionist's energetic mind prison,

7. Eliminate the fear of death,

8. Unleash their super human potential, (to be discussed later)

9. Increase their desire for life,

10. Activate their legacy in life,

11. Reveal their energetic role and purpose in life,

12. Unleash spontaneous healing,

13. Maximize self-awareness,

14. Maximize enlightenment,

15. Recognize and understand their past lives,

16. Understand their between lives downloads from their previous activations with the violet energy force of Quantum Consciousness,

17. Make their transformation into Quantum Consciousness experience real,

18. Increase self-respect,

19. Eliminate pain, fear and insecurity,

20. Maximize wisdom,

21. Access their all-knowingness of everything,

22. Increase energy,

23. Unleash past unknown memories,

24. Complete and fulfill their life.

During your activations of transformation there is no gravitational force to hold your soul down, no sense of time to break up your soul's reactivation with Quantum Consciousness and no physical sensations. You feel no pain, temperature, or fatigue. Your soul is simply led to its reactivation with the violet energy force of Quantum Consciousness.

Activations of transformation usually encounter other soul fragments of who you were in past lives that have become blocked and stuck in their energetic travels and journey back to Quantum Consciousness. These are energies from your past lives that must be set free. Many times others have experienced profound improvements to their health when these soul fragments are set free. Some have met loved ones who have passed away during their activations of transformation. Some have met historical figures during their activations of transformation. No two activations of transformation are ever the same.

Here is a copy of an email I received from Mike, after his first activation of transformation session I had with him.

"I felt my body start to lift off the bed moving to the right side of me then hovering about one foot above the bed at the level of the light. I saw the light turn into what looked like the center of the galaxy with bright striations emanating all over. At that point my hands became tight and started vibrating as if a power surge was going through them. I then began to feel extremely warm ... when I opened my eyes then closed them again I saw what looked like the photo negative of everything in the room including myself and for a brief moment I could even see the skeletal bones in my hands and arms as if I was looking at an x-ray. I then felt a brief moment of peace and happiness come over me and I started to laugh as if on a drug (but not on a drug). I haven't felt like that for a long long time."

Here is some email correspondence I received from Becky during her activation of transformation sessions I was having with her.

It began with the following email:

Hi JC,

Something has come to mind about that session.

Do you remember when I was at the chalk board and I said "I think it's a flower?" The reason I said "I think" is because of the way I drew it. Normally, I would draw a flower like the image of Flower A that I have attached to this email. But the way I drew it is as per the image of Flower B. Do you see the difference in the way the petals were drawn in these 2 images?

Image A: Image B:

 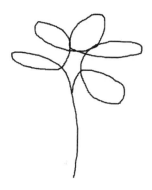

In image A, the petals were drawn down and around. In image B, they were drawn up and then they cross down over themselves. This indicates that, when I'm teaching, my higher self takes over and directs the flow of information.

My response to her email was as follows:

This is profound.

Thanks for sharing.

What I see in diagram B is you soaring and flying. The petals representing your head, arms and legs and are connected to your body. Your arms and legs are acting as your wings. This is an image of your transformation with the force. (like a flying turtle).

I must admit that the image you drew within the box on the board has been on my mind. This revelation you have given me about the flower has provided me with a possible missing element.

Let me know how this resonates with you.

Closing in the box around the images clearly closes off the message. I know the message is about you (and all of humanity).

When trying to comprehend what this means, I am impressed that the proper way to understand this is to read it like a pyramid, from the middle then to the left and then the right.

House represents your absolute security and absolute value.

The big heart is your physical realm absolute and represents the first half of the equation the soaring flower is your spiritual realm absolute and represents the second half of the equation.

So your drawings are speaking to me this way.

The complete you is secure, safe and valuable and is the answer to the equation of who Becky energetically is. For you to be your complete secure self it is the combination of your complete physical realm self that will produce the massive big heart, eliminate all fears and securities and produce your physical realm purity and Quantum Consciousness self.

Your drawing is the equation of your transformation into the violet energy force of Quantum Consciousness within you and also is your energetic absolutes of the force's energetic perfection and perfect love.

Your drawing is energetically what we all are and our life energies, energetic ultimate purpose and potential for living this life experience.

From a mathematical perspective I am impressed this is our energetic formula of who we are. The formula is the following:

$.001 + 99.999 = 100.$

House is 100 or 100% of energetic absolute of who we are and our ultimate potential. (also all of humanity).

99.999 is the soaring flower or 99.999% your activations of transformation produce.

Humanity has done life only accessing .001% of their potential in physical realm.

It will be amazing as 100% absolutes work together and unleash the complete energetic transformation of Quantum Consciousness.

Have you just seen the energetic pictogram for the limitless potential of humanity?

Thank you for sharing.

JC

All activation of transformation sessions begin with the removal of all physical realm energies. It is only your Theta brainwave rhythm speed that can access this state. If slowing your mind down to access its Theta brainwave rhythm speed is a problem I have found that taking 1 tablespoon of liquid magnesium 30 minutes prior to the beginning of your activation of transformation sessions helps calm the mind down.

Everyone who has completed their activations of transformation has told me it significantly enhanced their life. It provided the hope, meaning and purpose to their life many thought was impossible to access. Some have told me it has left them speechless with new feelings and insights of bliss, love, freedom, abundance and wisdom that they had not previously had. Everyone has unlocked the door of the illusionist's energetic mind prison and no longer see the world through the energetic blinders they were wearing while stuck in the illusionist's energetic mind prison. Many found their activations of transformation have unleashed new, specialized knowledge and wisdoms to them which they had not previously known.

You can never go through your activations of transformation if you are afraid of new ideas, or if you suffer from indecision, doubt, worry, caution, procrastination or hoarding. One simply cannot communicate with Quantum Consciousness with any fear and negativity attached.

There are some who at this moment are experiencing an undeniable fluttering explosion or bubbling up feeling inside of them as you read. If this is you, please know this is an energetic signal of joy coming from your soul as it begins to awaken. It is your soul letting you know it is ready to be reactivated again with the violet energy force of Quantum Consciousness so that its evolution can be completed.

Activating the totality of Quantum Consciousness's energetic perfection and perfect love within you does not depend on anything except you. There are no favorites. Everyone has a violet energy thread of Quantum Consciousness locked away within them that has been waiting for this moment.

As children, we do not separate the possible from the impossible. This is why the younger a person's mind is the older their soul tends to be and the easier it is to re-activate and unleash the totality of Quantum Consciousness.

Science has proven energy cannot be destroyed. Hence, your soul and violet energy thread of Quantum Consciousness has never and never will be destroyed. Science realizes any energetic potential is released when a force acts upon it. Science refers to this force as a restoring force. Activations of transformation are your soul's restoring force that reactivates the energetic perfection and perfect love of Quantum Consciousness violet energy with your soul.

Activations of transformation begin by removing any and all energetic parasites and toxins that have caused energetic blockages in your soul. Cleansing your soul's energetic blockages is always the first step in everyone's activations of transformation.

To understand what can happen during activations of transformation sessions, one of my friends whom I shall call Mary, agreed to share her activations of transformation I had with her. Mary's activations of transformation took place over the telephone, while she was in the comfort of her home.

Mary's Activation of Transformation-session #1

Mary's first activation of transformation session began when she eliminated all of her physical realm energies. I knew Mary was in her Theta brainwave rhythm speed state when she said the gates to hell are always open and she is stuck and cannot move on.

Mary's soul revealed a globe out of which different streams, bells, rings, markings and points were sticking out. She knew these points were different life experiences from her many previous life experiences.

I asked Mary to look around as she began to travel deeper and see if any past soul fragments from past life experiences could be found. She quickly found a soul fragment reveal itself to her as Angra, whose family had been wiped out in an invasion when she was 22 years of age. Angra's husband and her babies were all slaughtered by men on horseback right before her eyes. This occurred during what she thought was the Mongol invasion.

Mary's past soul fragment of Angra was stuck in her soul. Due to the traumatic death she had experienced, and because of the loss of her husband and babies, Angra had trust issues with moving on. Ironically, Mary has constantly had trust issues manifest in her life as anguish, anger and sadness. I pointed Angra to the light of the spiritual realm which she had been trying to enter. Angra saw it. As she looked into it she saw her husband and her babies in the light with their arms held open, they were calling her to come home. Mary saw Angra go through the light and death portal and leave her soul.

Mary then had Dungrith come forward. He was a man of the woods, who could not release himself. He said, "I killed him. I'm not worthy. I killed my brother over a woman." When Dungrith was pointed to the light, he saw the door was open and waiting for him. Mary also saw him leave and go through the light.

Mary then saw Jacob from Jamaica. Mary's voice then spoke to me with a thick Jamaican accent. Jacob lived with nature. He had been taken in a boat by a white man who then sank the boat. Jacob never saw his family again. Jacob felt abandoned, alone and discontented. He knew he did not belong here but could not move on. Mary saw him leave quickly in a rocket, into the light.

This concluded Mary's first activation of transformation session. The total time was 2 hours.

I have since made it a practice to not exceed a 60 minute activation of transformation session with anyone. They are simply too energetically draining for the person experiencing them if they exceed 60 minutes.

Mary's Activation of Transformation-session #2
At Mary's second activation of transformation session, she entered into her Theta brainwave rhythm state again where she saw a glowing golden globe. Her golden globe was blocked like water at the edge of a dam. She said, "Golden globe is stuck, cannot move down." Mary knew this was a huge issue. She felt resigned to the

golden globe being stuck. I asked Mary to watch the globe. As she watched, the globe became brighter. It appeared to be getting closer to her very quickly.

As the golden globe moved closer, she saw a man who she was from a previous life experience. He revealed himself as Simon, a knight who had lived during the dark ages, before the Knights Templar. Simon had revealed the secrets to an artifact that was not supposed to be revealed and he had sworn to uphold. The artifact was part of a power that triggered DNA to yield instantaneous manifestations. The Sun was darkened as a result of Simon revealing this information. I pointed Simon towards the light, which overcame Simon's guilt for disclosing this secret.

Simon saw the light reaching out to him and he became one with it. He went into the light and is now home. Mary felt goose bumps when Simon went home. She said everyone was happy he was home.

Mary is an old soul who has a lot of light. This attracts dark ones who are monitoring her. When I asked Mary if there were any other's coming forward from within her soul, a non-human entity appeared and identified itself as Sondra, from planet 421. It said, "I am of a planet not of this universe." I asked Sondra how it had entered into the soul of Mary. I forcefully told the entity to leave Mary. Sondra said she was invited by Mary. Sondra said she and others had been using Mary to learn for the federation of planets. I asked Mary if she had sold her soul. Mary said she had only loaned her soul out. I had an intense battle with Sondra who did not want to leave. After about fifteen minutes Sondra eventually left the soul of Mary.

I asked Mary to look around and look for other entities to reveal themselves. But none appeared. Mary was energetically exhausted after this session.

Later, I received the following email from Mary.

Wow JC!

That was pretty amazing. I feel sooooo happy. Like my chest is one big balloon of happy.

I would like to reside in this forever. Suddenly everything has no importance. No feelings of resentment or painful memories. Nothing feels like it is sticking. I feel like I am in a healing place drawing in a rest period so that I will be more ready when the time is right to begin working...whatever that looks like. I have a sense my life is going to be very exciting and I have no idea doing what...although I suspect I will be helping people clear their blocks and will be able to see them more clearly.
THANK YOU THANK YOU THANK YOU.

It is a wonderful thing that you do.

Mary's Activation of Transformation-session #3

Before we started Mary's third activation of transformation session, she started to shake with excitement. Once she was in her Theta brainwave rhythm state this session began when I asked her what she saw. She again saw the golden globe, parts of which were moving like a river. This confirmed once again that Mary was in her Theta brainwave rhythm state.

Mary then saw a very bright light, which was much closer to her than it had been before. Being close to the light, she felt joy, peace and happiness. But she knew she was not ready to go through the light. She said there are others still trapped.

The next soul fragment that came forward identified himself as Luke. He was from the year 1789, the time of the Spanish explorers. Luke had explored down the east coast and in inlets, looking for gold. He was unable to return, became shipwrecked and died. He had been sleeping in a room and was suddenly trapped, there was water everywhere and he could not get out. He couldn't breathe.

Because he was scared, Luke could not go through the light. He did not want to go into the light. But when I told him to look up at the light, he was able to move into it very quickly. When he passed through the light, he was greeted by two voices that both Mary and myself audibly heard greet him.

Next, Mary saw Joshua who was known as Nick. Nick was a 10 year old crippled boy who had been murdered and was confused. After much delay, I was led to tell him what had taken place during his life was not his fault. He said he should have listened and not gone into the darkness. When I told him to go to the light, he went through it.

Mary's soul now confirmed to her she did not have any more soul fragments or invaders stuck in her soul. I then instructed Mary to move forward into the light which she did.

Through the light Mary could see miles and miles of amazing, flower filled landscape. She sat down on a cliff, far removed from anything and everyone.

She immediately saw her Old English sheepdog, Benji, whom she had missed very much. He was happy and full of energy. Together, they began walking toward a group of people.

Mary then saw a young girl. When she asked her who she was, Mary was told she was the daughter Mary did not have. She was the one who didn't live. She told Mary she was fine, but the energetic circumstances were not right for her to enter the physical realm. This gave Mary tremendous peace as she had always held this traumatic experience close to her heart. She had been punishing herself for many years for her failure to deliver this child.

Benji and Mary then began walking toward a village where many of her friends and relatives were waiting for her. These people included her parents, her grandparents and her uncle; all were happy and proud of her for making it here while still living. Everyone acknowledged her and encouraged her for what she was doing.

Suddenly, the sky was golden, the trees were like a tapestry, music was everywhere and there was no blackness. She heard a voice. We waited for about 10 minutes. But no one came. Then she saw flowers everywhere. She knew the flowers were the energy from the Quantum Consciousness of God. They said, "I am the Quantum Consciousness of God. The only plan for you is with me."

The total time was 2 hours. Mary sent me the following message the day after her third activation of transformation session.

Hello JC,

These are just thoughts which have come to me in the aftermath of our session...

The two aspects...one which died in a shipwreck (Luke?) and (Joshua/Nick) both of these died with lung issues. Luke by drowning and Nick with a knife to the chest. I am wondering if my breathing will get easier with their release. I also found that I actually felt a physical evacuation when they left, like a movement of energy being pulled out of the physical body.

Am also somewhat annoyed about Benji, the dog. I have cried over that stupid dog more times than anyone else in my life. I mourn him over and over and it doesn't seem to finish...although it gets further away with time.

Whenever I see an old English sheepdog, I just turn to fluff and think about him. I guess he is the closest thing (or the real thing) to unconditional love I have ever had in this lifetime.

I had a very wakeful night last night as I was high on energy.

You will see a picture of my Benji attached. He was big, fluffy and very sweet!

Thank you again, I appreciate it VERY MUCH!

Mary

Mary's dog Benji

Mary's Activation of Transformation-session #4

To begin Mary's fourth activation of transformation session, she entered into her Theta brainwave rhythm speed. At this time, she heard sounds, like a humming or a heartbeat. Then she went through the light and saw a city near the bottom of a hill. The city was crystal and bright. Sounds were coming from it. Mary saw it to be magnificent and beautiful. The crystal had many colors. Within the city was one main building that had glass and marble in front of it. She was amazed at the art patterns in the rock. The patterns were making sounds as if they were alive. She pushed down on a handle on the door of the building and walked inside.

The inside of the building was as bright as the outside. The light was emanating from the pure energetic perfection and perfect love of God's violet energy Quantum Consciousness force. Mary felt honored to be in its presence. She was very happy to be with the energy of Source. She was next led to a room that was bare. Mary felt it to be a place of worship. There were eleven men in this room, 4 of whom were sitting on the floor. There was nothing else in this room; it did not need anything else. She was told that few arrive here while alive in the physical realm, she was on a long journey and this was the stepping-stone in her journey.

Now Mary's soul entered its deepest stage. She felt an awareness she had not felt before. She was told it would increase her vibrations and her consciousness. She was told to call certain people forward into a group to activate and unleash their souls. She was told she needed to be cleared and prepared to go forward and help support those in this regard. The unleashing of Mary's Quantum Consciousness self and super human state had begun.

At this point, I helped Mary reactivate her soul with the violet energy of Quantum Consciousness. Mary was impressed this meant profound events were about to unfold in her life. She was ready to open and reveal incredible synchronicity through her Quantum Consciousness and super human self. Mary indicated this was all she wanted to do and this is why she is alive today. She has no will but to do what Quantum Consciousness reveals.

Mary then found herself within a courtyard where a man approached her from the courtyard gates. He was dressed in attire from biblical times. Mary noticed she was also dressed the same way. The man greeted her as an old friend and told her a group of people had been waiting for her and had agreed to come forward. Then the group surrounded her. The man reminded Mary it must become her priority to dissolve her ego and this must occur before more events can be revealed to her. She was further revealed this experience awaits everyone and will impact all of humanity. This is not a task, but rather, a quest. The initiative produces the outcome.

The total time for this activation of transformation session was 2 hours.

This completed Mary's activations of transformation and reactivated her soul with the totality of Quantum Consciousness's violet energy force.

To this day, I continue to assist Mary as she unleashes her Quantum Consciousness limitless potential and transfigures her body and mind sub atomically into the violet energy of Quantum Consciousness.

It became apparent to me during my post NDE journey that prior to one's activations of transformation no one has experienced their true potential in life - physically, emotionally, mentally, spiritually, relationally or financially. This is because they have not re-activated their soul with Quantum Consciousness and they have not transformed its violet energy within them to unleash their limitless potential.

One client described it this way, "I've found my Jeannie in a bottle and all I have to do is actualize its leading."

It is amazing how the transformation of Quantum Consciousness begins to work in a person. Many have told me they have an enhanced love, relationship and understanding about life and everything that is associated with it like they have never had before. Some people experience an enhancement to their vertical multi-dimensional reality in phenomenal ways. Some have suddenly begun to see multi-dimensional energy and auras around life similar to Kirlian photography.

155 / AWAKEN THE FORCE

Human Energy as seen through Kirlian Photography:

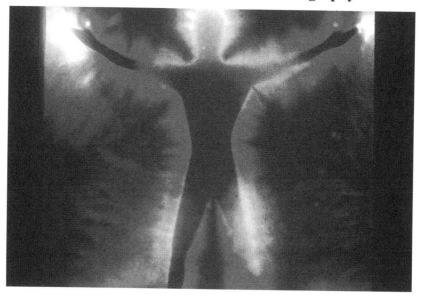

Some people begin to see multi-dimensional energy in the air, where previously nothing was seen before. Some begin to see the colors of multi-dimensional energy actually move in and out of the minds of people. Others have picked up the vibrations of energy from living objects. Some pick up the thoughts of others and know what a person is going to say and do before they do it. Some even notice an enhanced sense of touch as they feel multi-dimensional energy in a way which is totally new to anything they have previously felt. Some can see, feel and understand the energy of others and what it is doing to them. For most, their dreams become more meaningful, real and profound.

Prior to my NDE, Jesus, Buddha, Moses and Elijah were the only humans who had ever completed their activations of transformation with the totality of Quantum Consciousness in the physical realm. This unleashed their limitless potential and transfigured their bodies and minds to complete their ascension. Jesus talked about what happens after activations of transformation this way, *"Don't you believe that I am in the Father, and that the Father is in me? The words I say to you I do not speak on my own authority. Rather, it is the Father, living in me, who is doing his work."* John 14:10. Jesus referred to God as the Father whenever he spoke so the masses could easily grasp his meaning. The masses had not completed their activations of transformation and could not have understood that he was talking about the violet energy force of Quantum Consciousness and mind of God so he spoke in parables and simplified his message to what it was.

However, there was a time in the lives of Jesus, Buddha, Moses and Elijah when their souls had not re-activated with the totality of Quantum Consciousness. Energetically their Beta state of mind was no different than your Beta state of mind is today. Like you, they needed to complete their activations of transformation with Quantum Consciousness before their souls could be re-activated with it. Their body and mind's subatomic energy was not transfigured into the violet energy force of Quantum Consciousness's energetic perfection and perfect love until they had completed their activations of transformation with the totality of Quantum Consciousness. As a result all 4 were able to ascend their body and mind's.

Activations of transformation are the only way to complete your soul's evolution and transfigure your mind and body into the energetic perfection and perfect love of Quantum Consciousness. This is exactly what Jesus, Buddha. Moses and Elijah experienced.

Your body and minds transfiguration into the violet energy energetic perfection and perfect love of Quantum Consciousness begins immediately after you complete your activations of transformation.

18

Super Humanity

"There comes a time when the mind takes a higher plane of knowledge"

Albert Einstein

After completing your activations of transformation the totality of Quantum Consciousness's violet energy force of energetic perfection and perfect love will be re-activated again with your soul.

Your soul will no longer be a separate and isolated violet energy thread of Quantum Consciousness trapped within your body. It is no longer subject to a Gilligan like existence. It has been rescued from its deserted island and re-activated with the totality of Quantum Consciousness.

Alive and well within you the violet energy force of Quantum Consciousness can now begin to transfigure its energetic perfection and perfect love to your mind and body.

Now as the absolute power of Quantum Consciousness your soul is no longer a separate and isolated violet energy thread of Quantum Consciousness like it has always been in all of its past life experiences in the physical realm. You authorized Quantum Consciousness to unleash its violet energy power of energetic perfection and perfect love to your body and mind when you completed your activations of transformation.

Before you were born, your soul carried out its life energy contract with Quantum Consciousness and injected your body and mind's atoms with the red, green and blue strong force energy of Quantum Consciousness to empower your survival. Sub atomically the energy of your body and mind's atoms has always been the red, green and blue strong force energy of Quantum Consciousness.

This was the same for the fab 4 who also needed to reactivate their souls with the violet energy force of Quantum Consciousness. Their completed activations of transformation was how they transformed into the energetic perfection and perfect love of Quantum Consciousness in the physical realm. They also authorized their body and mind's red, green and blue subatomic energy to be transfigured into the violet energy of Quantum Consciousness. This not only completed their souls evolution it led to the unleashing of their limitless potential. This could not have happened without their soul being reactivated with Quantum Consciousness through their activations of transformation.

The energetic perfection and perfect love of Quantum Consciousness transfigured the fab 4's body and mind's red, green and blue sub atomic energy to their energetic perfection and perfect love violet energy force totality of Quantum Consciousness. This is how and why their ascension happened. It is also how and why your ascension will happen.

However, before the fab 4's ascension they experienced a temporary state of super humanity. Their temporary state of super humanity was their Quantum Consciousness limitless potential while they lived prior to their ascension. They became the violet energy force of Quantum Consciousness that manifested itself as their soul's ultimate wisdom, their body's ultimate wellness and their mind's ultimate wealth. The fab 4's state of super humanity transfigured their mind, body and soul into the energetic perfection and perfect love of Quantum Consciousness while they lived.

My post NDE journey inspired me that anyone's state of super humanity can be unleashed during the 70 year transformation. The time of now is when anyone can unleash their bionic state of super humanity.

Today's 70 years of transformation is the battle of Armageddon. Armageddon is the site of gathering armies for a last day battle between good and evil. Until now it has not been known if Armageddon is a literal site or a symbolic location. Armageddon has been a term used in a generic sense to refer to any end of the world scenario.

Spiritual interpretation of Armageddon is the Messiah will return to Earth and defeat the Antichrist. The Messiah is the force and violet energy totality of Quantum Consciousness that entered the physical realm on December 21, 2012 at 11:11:11 GMT at the energetic unlocking of the fifth energy seal. The Antichrist is the energy of evil that has been in the physical realm since the opening of the fourth energy seal 13.75 billion years ago. It has controlled and manipulated the minds of humanity and placed them into energetic mind prisons.

It was during my post NDE journey that I was further inspired that the battle of Armageddon will not be a physical battle; rather, it will be an energetic battle that takes place in the minds' of humanity. The mind is the energetic battle ground for the battle of Armageddon between the energies of good and evil.

The energies of the Messiah will meet the energies of the Antichrist in the minds of humanity. This battle began on December 21, 2012. The dark force energy of the Antichrist has always controlled our minds. It was released into the physical realm at the energetic unlocking of the fourth energy seal when the pale lightning bolt unleashed an energetic power to control and manipulate humanity. The energy of the Messiah was released to the physical realm at the energetic unlocking of the fifth energy seal on December 21, 2012. It too must enter your mind in order for your energetic battle of Armageddon to commence. This is what the completion of your activations of transformation will allow to happen.

The word Messiah is the spiritual term of energetic goodness. It is the Quantum Consciousness of God's energetic perfection and perfect love. It was the energy the fab 4 re-activated with that first produced their state of super humanity and ultimately their ascension.

The word Antichrist is the spiritual term of energetic evil. Energetically, the pale lightning bolt unleashed this energy at the energetic unlocking of the fourth energy seal 13.75 billion years ago to create the energy of fear and negativity. This energy has acted as the checks and balance and energetic "devil's advocate" in God's mastermind plan of life.

Therefore, the minds of humanity and your mind must choose what energy it wishes to become. Will it choose super humanity, ascension and your limitless potential or will it choose death, destruction and decay? This is everyone's choice in the energetic battle of Armageddon.

The energetic battle of Armageddon is all about choice. Energetically, it is the foundational choice everyone who is alive today must make. Will you choose death, destruction and decay as your body, mind and soul's ultimate energy or will you choose to become the violet energy force and totality of Quantum Consciousness. This is the choice your mind must make in the energetic battle of Armageddon.

The choice of what your mind chooses is best for you is yours and only yours to make. Either you remain caught up in your ego based choices of life or you eliminate ego and unleash the energetic perfection and perfect love of Quantum Consciousness's violet energy totality.

Ever since humanity first appeared on the planet we have needed, accepted and craved the emotion of love. Love is unquestionably our greatest emotion. Human nature is such that, the more love we give and receive, the more fulfilled, content and satisfied we become.

Our need for love was first realized in the womb with the flow of hormones we received from our mothers. This flow continued after birth as we were nursed and loved by our parents. Studies have shown children who grow up deprived of love become fundamentally crippled, both physically and psychically. It has been shown that a disruption of love affects the well being of children. These children tend to die sooner than those who do not have a disruption of love.

Over the last 100 years, the illusionist through his ambition to numb humanity through his drug of money and satisfy our egos has significantly manipulated our energetic pendulum of love. This is confirmed by reviewing our energetic pendulum of love.

Between the years 1912 and 1918 our energetic pendulum of love fell because of World War I. The so-called causes of World War I included many intertwined factors, such as the conflicts and hostility of diplomatic clashes during the 5 preceding decades, which changed the balance of power in Europe. These were some of the illusionist's earliest ways in which he provoked war.

World War I started in the summer of 1914 and mobilized more than 70,000,000 military personnel, including 60,000,000

Europeans. World War I was responsible for the deaths of over 9,000,000 combatants. This was a time when humanity did nothing but survive. In comparison to earlier years, it produced a very low energetic level of love.

After World War I, the energetic pendulum of love began to rise. Families were reunited; they began to focus on rebuilding and providing love through the family unit. However, this was short lived as the roaring twenties moved on to produce a break in traditions.

By the end of the 1920's, the literal measured realities of humanity seemed to revolve around the external stimuli of new technologies which were being developed. New technologies, such as automobiles, moving pictures and radio were introduced to the majority of the population. Externally to our consciousness, life appeared to be booming until the ego and its desire for excesses began to rear its ugly head again thanks to money. However, as the 1920s came to an end, the energetic pendulum of love began to fall again. A marked decline in social consciousness and love was prevalent primarily because of the impact money was having in people's lives. Money was pulling people away from the love of family to the love of the excesses money was creating.

Then came the Great Depression, which started primarily because of money. Unlike World War I there was no war to drive down the energetic pendulum of love. But the events that were orchestrated around the great depression did.

Scholars on this subject believe the stock market crash which occurred on October 29, 1929 was the first major cause of the Great Depression. Within 2 months, investors had lost more than 40 billion dollars or the equivalent of 24 trillion dollars today. The illusionist had again vaporized net worth. Even though the stock market began to regain some of its losses by the end of 1930 the Great Depression had begun.

Another cause of the Great Depression was bank failures. Throughout the 1930's over 9000 banks failed in the United States. Bank deposits were uninsured and as banks failed, people simply lost their savings as the illusionist began to take back what was his.

In the 1930's the surviving banks were rightfully very concerned about their own survival, they stopped issuing new loans, which only exacerbated the situation. A reduction in purchasing power began and people stopped purchasing items. This, in turn, created a reduction in the workforce.

When people lost their jobs, they were unable to maintain the payments on the items they had purchased through installment plans. Subsequently, those items were repossessed. More inventories began to accumulate and the unemployment rate rose. Does this sound familiar? Yes, it's happening again today.

To protect local businesses, governments began to charge high tariffs on foreign goods, which led to countries retaliating against each other economically. Again, the culprit was money. But, this time the lack of money produced a significant downturn in the energetic pendulum of love. Downturns in the energetic pendulum of love produce mass unexpected calamities.

World War II was no different. This was a period in history when, energetically, life was again about survival. Again, the energetic pendulum of love moved downward and bottomed out at the end of World War II.

By the end of World War II, society began to move the energetic pendulum of love back in an upward direction. This peaked in 1964 as men and women married and raised children during the baby boomer generation from 1946-1964. During this time, children received the love they required. Today's baby boomers can all remember their youth. They remember how they used to play outside all day, ride bikes, build forts and make up games. They had few fears and insecurities.

For the most part, the baby boomer generation lived in the same house, went to the same schools and retained the same friends throughout their childhood. At this time, there was rarely ever a need for people to lock the doors of their homes because the emotions of fear and insecurity virtually did not exist.

The energetic pendulum of love began to gravitate downward again in 1965. This was when the average household income began to rise. Since this time household incomes have risen by 880%. This has produced the fastest growth rate ever and is due to the emergence of the two-income family. The two-income family meant parents no longer had the time to give their children the love and support they required. Studies have shown today parents spend an average of 3 1/2 minutes per week participating in meaningful conversations with their children.

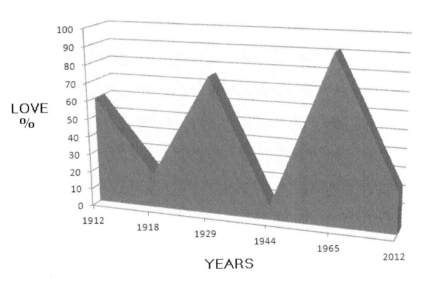

The Energetic Love of Humanity

Two-income families relied on technology to make life manageable. This forced children to rely on technology for play. This limited both their creativity and their physical development. This limitation resulted in the fundamental crippling of today's children, producing new neurological and developmental problems which rarely existed among children of the baby boomer generation. This includes learning disabilities, autism, sensory processing disorder, developmental coordination disorder, anxiety disorder and depression, to name a few. Only 30 years ago 1 in 50,000 children was diagnosed with autism. Today, this ratio is 1 in 110.

Depression is also at the forefront. The affects of depression are being felt everywhere like never before. Take professional sports as an example. Recently, the retired baseball player, Hideki Irabu, committed suicide at the young age of 42, because of depression. Within a 3 month period during the summer of 2011 ice hockey suffered 3 tragedies. First, Derek Boogaard committed suicide at the age of 31. Next, Rick Rypien committed suicide at the age of 27; then it was Wade Belak who committed suicide at the age of 35. All of these suicides were caused by depression and all of these victims were in the age group where the underlying cause might very well have been a lack of love during their childhood. We can only hope this is not the start of a depression induced suicide epidemic among this age demographic.

For nearly fifty years, technology has become the primary parent and babysitter to our children. This technological connection has produced in them an energetic disconnect. Today, as children develop and form identities they are often incapable of discerning whether they are a killing machine, as is demonstrated in some video games, or just a shy and lonely little child in need of a friend.

As children, baby boomers survived by creating and playing out their dreams. Today's children are now under the assumption they need technology in order to survive. However, technology cannot provide the love children desire and need. As a result, these children have developed an artificial love, or dependence, on technology.

Today these children are searching for their fundamental need of love in the best way they know, through technology, primarily using the Internet. This is why social networking sites are so popular. Today's social networking phenomenon is aimed primarily at those aged fifty and younger. It can be credited back to the lack of love which developed through the technologically parented generation beginning in 1965. The roots of most social networking sites started as nothing more than a cry for help from this love-starved generation of children born after 1965. They are searching for love the best way they know how - through technology and the Internet. As a result, the energetic love pendulum is approaching record lows again today.

This love-starved generation can be seen even more in large urban centers, where the devastating phenomenon of second generation children from technological parenting is everywhere. These are the children who grew up with parents who were themselves starved of love by their technological parents. Today, many of these second generation, technologically parented children are traumatized, even before they enter school. More and more of these children are living in a world where the absence of parental love has produced children who live their day-to-day existence without hope. Many are even incapable of giving or receiving love.

The lack of love permeating society today has grown to epidemic proportions. This combined with the looming financial crisis is a prescription for an unmitigated disaster and something the Antichrist and its dark force energy of fear and negativity is in the midst of attempting to implement. The Antichrist is purposely moving us towards a broken, barren, loveless society. His goal is to turn first world nations into third world nations and he is accomplishing this by eliminating the middle class. The unleashing of Quantum Consciousness's energetic perfection and perfect love has never been more needed than it is today.

In God's mastermind plan of life its Quantum Consciousness is pre-destined to be unleashed into every one of the Universe's atoms. Why? Because it is only the violet energy force of Quantum Consciousness that can be energetically birthed as God's infinite, eternal energetic body at the completion of Quantum Consciousness's Omega energy strand.

How the totality of Quantum Consciousness is to be unleashed into every one of the Universe's atoms was revealed by both Jesus and Buddha. Jesus spoke about it this way *"Love the Lord your God with all your heart and with all your soul and with all your mind. This is the first and greatest commandment. And the second is like it: Love your neighbor as yourself."* Matthew 22:37-39. Buddha spoke about it this way, *"You, yourself, as much as anybody in the entire universe, deserve your love and affection."*

Combined, Jesus and Buddha revealed love triangles between the Quantum Consciousness of God, yourself and any other energy aspect. It will be through love triangles that the totality of God's violet energy Quantum Consciousness can be re-activated into every single atom in the Universe.

Triangles have 3 sides and 3 angles that always add up to 180 degrees. Triangles protect and lock in anything that is within its 3 sides. Therefore, it is the love triangles between the Quantum Consciousness of God, your soul and any other energy aspect that will re-activate the violet energy totality of Quantum Consciousness into every one of the Universe's atoms.

Prayer and meditation is how mankind has requested help from God, given thanks to God or induced a state of mind that brings a person closer to God. Energetically, traditional prayer and meditation has been a finite limiting request usually for the benefit of the individual who made the prayer or who meditated. They have not had the energetic depth of love triangles to maximize their effectiveness.

The combination of prayer and medication with love triangles makes a person's prayer and meditation much more effective. It's like driving a car from point A to point B. To get to point B from point A you must drive the roads that take you from point A to point B. In prayer or meditation the energetic roads from point A to point B are energy's superstrings and if you haven't included energy in your prayer or meditation it's like trying to drive from point A to point B without driving on the roads that get you there.

Love triangles are your prayer and meditations energetic roadway that must be included with your prayer or meditation in order for your prayers or meditation to be the most effective they can be. This is also how the violet energy totality of Quantum Consciousness will be activated into all of the Universe's atoms.

Here's how to combine your love triangles of prayer and meditation to literally take them through the energetic stratosphere. First before praying or meditating create the 3 points of your love triangle. The 3 points of your love triangle are made up of your soul, the Quantum Consciousness of God and any other third energetic aspect. Your love triangle is a power of 3 that locks in all the energy of your love triangle within your 3 points.

Next visualize delivering your love triangle and all of its energy to the Quantum Consciousness of God's mind. This is where I was delivered to during my NDE. A key component for love triangles is visualization. The visualization of your love triangle prayer and meditation being placed into the mind of God is imperative.

Most that have completed their activations of transformation use a post activation transformation prayer/meditation journal to keep track of the date and time of their love triangle prayer or meditation request for two reasons. First is to measure the result and second is to not double up and pray or meditate this love triangle request again. If a person prays or meditates a love triangle request a second time into the mind of God it could actually be pulled out.

A second prayer or meditation request of a love triangle could happen because either you want to dictate how God should work or you do not trust that God knows how to work. Either way you will be ridiculing the violet energy Quantum Consciousness and mind of God which potentially could nullify your initial prayer or meditation love triangle request. Constant visualization of your love triangles completing the energetic perfection and perfect love of God's Quantum Consciousness goes a long way in helping with the completion of your request.

The violet energy force and Quantum Consciousness of God can also be seen, felt and desired by others. It always produces an energetic radiance that shines through a person to others. It will inspire others to want to be around you. It will also motivate others to ask you about it and seek it out in their lives.

Upon completing your activations of transformation the Quantum Consciousness of God is accessible to receive your love triangle prayer and meditation requests. Every atom in the Universe must eventually be placed within the violet energy of God's Quantum Consciousness through prayer or meditation love triangles. This is to ensure that the violet energy energetic perfection and perfect love of God's Quantum Consciousness is the energy of every atom so that every one of the Universe's atoms can ascend onto the infinite, eternal energetic body of God.

By completing your activations of transformation Quantum Consciousness can begin to energetically unleash your state of super humanity. It will begin to unleash your body's ultimate wellness attribute. Your body's ultimate wellness is created as your atoms are transfigured into the violet energy of Quantum Consciousness. Your body's sub atomic transfiguration into Quantum Consciousness's violet energy slows down the aging process and reverses age related disease.

Science has attempted to confront the aging process and age related disease through our cells. Today, the Holy Grail of medicine is oxidative stress. Medicine understands oxidative stress is the trigger that causes aging and age related disease. Oxidative stress is a measure of your body's wear and tear; it's like the rusting of an engine. Everyone experiences oxidative stress from the oxygen we breathe. Your body combats oxidative stress by producing the antioxidant enzymes superoxide dismutase, glutathione and catalase, whose purpose is to gobble up the free radicals of oxidative stress before they damage your cells.

Oxidative stress increases daily as toxic free radicals overwhelm your enzymes. They wreak havoc by accelerating the aging process and age related disease. High levels of oxidative stress are associated with more than 200 diseases including Cancer, Heart Disease, Diabetes, Muscular Dystrophies, Liver Disease, Autism, Alzheimer's and Periodontal Disease.

For sometime science thought direct antioxidants such as Vitamin C and Vitamin E along with antioxidant rich foods were enough to halt oxidative stress and free radicals. However, these direct antioxidants only eliminate free radicals at a 1:1 ratio. Using direct antioxidants you would need to consume 87 glasses of wine a day, or 357 oranges a day, or 11 pounds of blueberries a day or 120 vitamin C tablets (500mg) a day to neutralize the amount of free radicals your body produces each and every day.

Science understands your body's wellness resides in the cells. It understands eliminating oxidative stress is your cells' best way to fight your body's aging process and age related disease. Fortunately there is a natural indirect antioxidant that has been proven to eliminate oxidative stress in your cells. It's a Nrf2 activator that is "... the only supplement clinically proven to reduce oxidative stress by an average of 40% slowing down the aging process to that of a 20 year old."

Enhancing your cells with this Nrf2 activator is your body's second safeguard to ultimate wellness. When combined with the violet energy totality of God's Quantum Consciousness that sub atomically transfigures your atoms red, green and blue energy to the violet energy Quantum Consciousness of God your body's ultimate wellness begins to be unleashed.

The completion of your activations of transformation also unleashes your mind's ultimate wealth attribute. Your mind's ultimate wealth attribute removes the dark force energy of the Antichrist from your energetic allotment of money and replaces it with the Quantum Consciousness of God's violet energy. Your Quantum Consciousness money potential is far greater than anything you could ever imagine.

As the illusion has shown, money is the Antichrist's dark force weapon that he uses through the illusionist and the illusionist's money matrix. The Antichrist uses money to control and manipulate humanity. By completing your activations of transformation you are authorizing the Quantum Consciousness of God to remove the Antichrist's dark force energy from your allotment of money and replace it with God's violet energy

Quantum Consciousness. This is huge in the energetic battle of Armageddon because it significantly weakens the strength of the Antichrist.

Since 2008 the Antichrist has pulled money out of society and forced many to struggle financially like never before. Because of this many have been forced to survive with much less which has created problems that did not previously exist. This is the goal of the Antichrist.

As the totality of Quantum Consciousness begins to transfigure itself within your mind it will eliminate your ego. Ego is an issue that exists because of the red, green and blue subatomic energy in your minds atoms. Ego, Edges God Out. It is not only your mind that has edged God out it is also your energetic allotment of money that has edged God out because it too has been controlled by the Antichrist's dark force energy of fear and negativity.

It is your minds new subatomic force of Quantum Consciousness violet energy that provides the energetic authorization for Quantum Consciousness to energetically transmute itself into your energetic allotment of money. Your decision to complete your activations of transformation is the catalyst for this to happen. Because you have allowed the violet energy force of Quantum Consciousness to eliminate ego, Quantum Consciousness can also eliminate the dark force energy of the Antichrist from your energetic allotment of money.

The false intent of money first appeared on the US 2 cent coin in 1864 and was first circulated on US paper currency on October 1, 1957. It reads "In God we Trust". It gave the impression that money trusts God. This was placed on money by the illusionist to falsely make it appear that money is trusted by God. This could be no further from the energetic reality of money.

Your mind's new state of super humanity will no longer crave, hoard or identify with being attached to things. It unleashes a non attachment to things because your ego is eliminated. The elimination of your ego also removes your fear and insecurity that previously only your attachment to money could satisfy.

Do we need money to survive? Of course we do, this will never change. However, with the completion of your activations of transformation your mind's new ultimate wealth attribute energetically empowers your energetic allotment of money to flow to you from the energetic perspective of Quantum Consciousness energetic perfection and perfect love and not from the Antichrist's dark force energy of fear and negativity.

During my post NDE journey I was inspired with the soul awakening strategy (SAS) that transmutes the Quantum Consciousness of God's energetic perfection and perfect love into a person's energetic allotment of money. This is the re-energizing of money and is available to anyone who authorizes it. It monetarily rewards those who have completed their activations of transformation and helps others complete their activations of transformation.

SAS produces the divine aid and violet energy currency of Quantum Consciousness. Quantum Consciousness will re-energize money to become its violet energy currency. When the dominant energy in money becomes the Quantum Consciousness of God the power of the Antichrist weakens in the energetic battle of Armageddon.

SAS will produce divine aid philanthropists. Divine aid philanthropists will endow humanity through Quantum Consciousness's violet energy currency. Quantum Consciousness's violet energy currency will be used for the betterment of humanity by its divine aid philanthropists.

Money is the energetic root of all evil. Imagine what removing it from money will do. Imagine a world with no fear and insecurity. Imagine a world where it is not about what a person can do but rather about who a person is. Imagine a world where it is led by the Quantum Consciousness of God and not about the evil dollars and cents create. Imagine a world of peace with nothing to kill or die for. Imagine a world sharing and living as one with no greed or hunger. Eliminating the dark force energy of the Antichrist from money and replacing it with the Quantum Consciousness of God's energetic perfection and perfect love is pre-destined to become today's reality in God's mastermind plan of life.

Your state of super humanity is pre-destined in God's mastermind plan of life. Your body and mind's super humanity is what your soul has been longing to achieve for *your* body and mind in all of its life experiences.

Your soul is here in this, its final life experience; to not only complete its evolution onto the infinite, eternal energetic body of God but also to fulfill your body and minds state of super humanity in the physical realm until ascension. It is your mind and body's state of super humanity that will help validate all of your souls past life experiences of pain and suffering. This is your limitless potential.

It's only your ego that can stop your soul and the Quantum Consciousness of God's energetic perfection and perfect love from unleashing its limitless potential in you and into your energetic allotment of money.

19

The Hundredth Monkey Tipping Point

During my post NDE journey I was like a sponge seeking information and knowledge that would help me communicate the Quantum Consciousness of God in the most effective way.

I recall two non-related tidbits of information that always stuck with me; they were the hundredth monkey effect and the tipping point. They stayed with me because I was impressed they were meant to somehow help me to effectively communicate the Quantum Consciousness of God.

I came across the tipping point in Malcolm Gladwell's debut book, The Tipping Point: How Little Things Can Make a Big Difference.

In his book, Gladwell defines the tipping point as "critical mass, the threshold, the boiling point". He further states that the tipping point is reached when "ideas, products, messages and behaviors spread like viruses"

I was particularly intrigued with the tipping point because I sensed there would come a point in time when the Quantum

Consciousness of God will reach its tipping point. This will be the moment in time when Quantum Consciousness reaches its critical mass, threshold and boiling point and spreads faster than the speed of light to the minds of humanity. At this tipping point in time Quantum Consciousness's violet energy force will instantaneously enter all of humanity and change everyone's energetic disposition from mind, body and soul to soul, mind and body.

The hundred monkey effect is a studied phenomenon in which a new behavior spreads rapidly by unexplained means from one group to all related groups once a critical number or tipping point has been reached. The theory behind the hundredth monkey effect originated with Lawrence Blair and Lyall Watson in the mid to late 1970's who claimed it from Japanese scientists.

The account is that unidentified Japanese scientists conducted a study of macaque monkeys on the Japanese island of Koshima in 1952. These scientists observed that some of these monkeys learned to wash sweet potatoes and gradually this new behavior spread through the younger generation of monkeys. The researchers observed that once a critical number of monkeys were reached-the so-called hundredth monkey - this previously learned behavior instantly spread across the water to macaque monkeys on nearby islands. In other words the minds of macaque monkeys on the other islands knew how and why to wash sweet potatoes without ever witnessing it. Energetically it became an instinctual aspect of the macaque monkeys DNA on other islands.

The greatest mystery I had during my post NDE journey was what would trigger the hundredth monkey tipping point and instantly change the energetic disposition of humanity. What would the hundredth monkey tipping point event be that produces the Quantum Consciousness of God's critical mass, threshold and boiling point to instantaneously change humanity's energetic disposition from mind, body and soul to soul, body and mind.

This moment in time will be profound because no longer will the individual soul need to override the mind to let go and stop being manipulated by the illusion of life. No longer will the mind be controlled by ego and no longer will logic be a person's guiding light. This point in time will be the mass hundredth monkey tipping point in time when the energetic disposition of humanity instantly changes from mind, body and soul to soul, body and mind.

Humanity's mass hundredth monkey tipping point will happen because of science's weak force of nature that was unleashed by the pale lightning bolt at the energetic unlocking of the fourth energy seal 13.75 billion years ago. It will be through this weak force of nature that the energetic disposition of humanity will instantly change from mind, body and soul to soul, mind and body and eradicate ego from the mind. But what would be its trigger?

Then I remembered the hundredth monkey effect and tipping point was identified to me through my NDE energy zings. My NDE energy zings identified this moment during the energetic unlocking of the seventh energy seal, which is the time of now that began on December 21, 2012 at 11:11:13 GMT. It will be when 144,000 individuals are energetically sealed as the Quantum Consciousness of God. The sealing of the 144,000 will produce the hundredth monkey tipping point. This is the event that will instantly trigger humanity's mass energetic disposition change from mind, body and soul to soul, body and mind.

A seal is an embossed emblem, figure, symbol or word used as attestation or evidence of authenticity. A sealing is when a seal has sealed or protected something to insure that its contents have not been tampered with or altered.

Quantum Consciousness's instantaneous sealing to all of humanity will be its violet energy energetic attestation and energetic evidence of authenticity that seals and protects humanity from the energy of the Antichrist so that it cannot tamper or alter them in any way. The hundredth monkey tipping point in time will be when 144,000 individuals have completed their activations of transformation and become the Quantum Consciousness of God's energetic perfection of perfect love. This is what will automatically trigger the instantaneous energetic disposition change within all of humanity from mind, body and soul to soul, body and mind.

SAS's first activations of transformation trigger point is the completion of its first 144,000 activations. This not only will instantaneously eliminate ego from humanity it will also eliminate the dark force energy of the Antichrist from money and effectively end the energetic battle of Armageddon.

20

The Final Days

Ironically, Christianity, the so called most popular religion in the world today, does not believe in the pre-existence and reincarnation of the soul. They believe the soul only has one chance or one kick at the can of life. This really baffled me.

What flabbergasted me the most was this position contradicted the teachings of Jesus whom Christianity is supposedly modeled after. Jesus confirmed this in Matthew 11:12-14 *"From the days of John the Baptist until now, the kingdom of heaven has been subjected to violence, and violent people have been raiding it. For all the Prophets and the Law prophesied until John. And if you are willing to accept it, he is the Elijah who was to come."*

Jesus himself understood the pre-existence and reincarnation of the soul, when he taught the soul of John the Baptist was also the soul of Elijah who had ascended several hundred years before. This also was prophesized in the bible from the book of Malachi 4:5, after Elijah's ascension, *"Behold I will send you Elijah the prophet, before the coming of the great and dreadful day of the Lord."*

Why would Christianity, the so called religion of Jesus, deny his teaching on reincarnation and pre-existence of the soul?

As I continued to struggle with this dichotomy I discovered that the Roman Church eliminated the pre-existence and reincarnation of the soul in 553 A.D. at the Second Council of Constantinople in a move to limit their follower's direct relationship with God. In doing so it also turned out to be a brilliant marketing move for the church. By eliminating the pre-existence and reincarnation of the soul it implied to the follower's of the church that the church is the sole conduit to God. This tightened the church's control and authority over its followers and proved to be the financial bonanza the church was hoping it would be. To this very day churches through their rules and regulations control and manipulate their followers by creating the false notion that it is only through them that their followers can directly connect with God.

It is when the 144,000 individuals are energetically sealed by the Quantum Consciousness of God's energetic perfection and perfect love that the hundredth monkey tipping point will instantly change the energetic disposition of humanity. It is at this instant that everyone's energetic disposition changes from mind, body and soul to soul, body and mind and ego is eliminated.

The violet energy totality of God's Quantum Consciousness entered the physical realm on December 21, 2012 at 11:11:11 GMT in order to complete its energetic perfection and perfect love not only to the body and minds of humanity but to the energy of every atom in the Universe. This means that all of the Universe's atoms, including the body and minds of humanity, have never had the privilege to become the Quantum Consciousness of God in the physical realm prior to December 21, 2012 at 11:11:11 GMT.

Presently there are 7.2 billion violet energy threads of Quantum Consciousness on the planet who are all here to complete their evolution through their final life experience. However, there is less than 70 years to accomplish this.

Too energetically aid in this massive undertaking science will play a vital role. Very soon science will discover God's energetic signature and Energetic Blueprint of life is the essence of every atom. When science discovers the energetic signature of God within the quarks and strong nuclear force of every atom it will signify that the 144,000 have been sealed and the energetic disposition of humanity has instantly changed from mind, body and soul to soul, body and mind. The discovery of God's Energetic Blueprint of life in every atom will also confirm the energetic battle of Armageddon is finished.

At this moment in time the Quantum Consciousness of God will be known, accepted and felt by every human being. Why? Because at this moment in time the superstrings that connect with the atoms of humanity will be energetically transfigured from red, green and blue to violet because of humanity's energetic disposition change from mind, body and soul to soul, body and mind. At this time, every superstring of energy that regulates life will be the violet energy Quantum Consciousness of God.

The instantaneous energetic disposition shift of humanity will transfigure every atoms superstring from red, green and blue to violet. At this moment in time activations of transformation will be happening at a feverish pitch. All of humanity will have had their soul awakened and been impressed to complete their activations of transformation immediately.

This will create an energetic excitement humanity has not known before. The 144,000 individuals who completed their activations of transformation will be prepared for this moment in time through SAS. This energetic phenomenon will not be isolated, it will happen globally in every country and the 144,000 individuals will be prepared for this explosion.

As the mass transformation of God's Quantum Consciousness re-activates itself into the minds of humanity the Antichrist's dark force energy of fear and negativity will be defeated. When Quantum Consciousness's energetic perfection of perfect love becomes the dominating energy within money and within humanity the Quantum Consciousness of God will wipe out the central bankers' computer programs and accounts. Instantly every single financial record and financial transaction will vaporize. This will obliterate the Antichrist's dark force energy from money and the illusion of life that the Antichrist created will energetically be completed. However, those sealed by the Quantum Consciousness of God will be safe because of their violet energy sealing.

The Antichrist's final stand will be the gathering of its remaining military firepower to fight against its perceived enemy that it will have no idea how to attack. The world will be in chaos, but those who have completed their activations of transformation will be sealed as the violet energy force of Quantum Consciousness. The Antichrist will not be able to touch or harm them.

At this time God's Quantum Consciousness will unleash storms and earthquakes in the areas where the Antichrist has strategically built his forces. In an instant the islands and mountains surrounding the Antichrist's forces will topple and disappear. At this same time the major cities and areas where the Antichrist is located will collapse.

At this moment in time humanity will be an energetically divided community with emotions running higher than this world has ever known before. There will be those who have completed their activations of transformation and energetically been sealed as the violet energy force of Quantum Consciousness and there will be those who have chosen not to complete their activations of transformation and are not sealed as the violet energy force of Quantum Consciousness. It will be the unfortunate souls who have chosen to not complete their activations of transformation that will be exposed to the acts of God's Quantum Consciousness force.

Fortunately trends today indicate that by the year 2050 in the United States less than 1 per cent of the population will be Christian. A similar decline in Christianity is happening throughout the world.

I was inspired that this is all part of God's energetic perfection and perfect love. Christians must allow their soul to awaken and accept the clear teachings of Jesus regarding reincarnation and pre-existence of the soul in order to reap the rewards from the Quantum Consciousness of God in their life.

Part 4

The Ascension

21

Lift Off

On December 21, 2082 at 11:11:12 GMT, Theta, the Quantum Consciousness of God's eighth energy seal will be energetically unlocked on God's Energetic Blueprint of life. It authorizes the mass ascension. This will also be the moment in time when ascension begins in all of God's other 100 trillion energetic cells.

The humanity equivalent within all of God's other 100 trillion energetic cells will also begin their ascension out of their physical realm equivalent scenarios because they too have been energetically sealed by the violet energy force of God's Quantum Consciousness.

Everyone who has completed their activations of transformation and has had the Quantum Consciousness of God re-activated and unleashed in them will ascend. This is what empowered the ascension of Jesus, Buddha, Moses and Elijah. It will include those who are alive at this moment in time and those who are not. Those who may have died prior to December 21, 2082 and completed their activations of transformation will awaken from their sleep and also become part of humanity's mass 2082 ascension.

When God's eighth energy seal is energetically unlocked everyone's energetic ticket of empowerment that powers their ascension happens because of the energetic subatomic violet energy sealing of their atoms. For those that have completed their activations of transformation, ascension will be their final event in the physical realm.

The energetic unlocking of Theta from God's Energetic Blueprint of life activates the Quantum Consciousness of God to gently begin the ascension process in all 100 trillion energetic cells. For humanity, they will be gently lifted off the ground as the energetic unlocking of Theta neutralizes the effects of gravity on those whose body and mind have become the subatomic violet energy force of Quantum Consciousness.

I was inspired that the purpose of my energetic preview during my NDE was to reveal the 2082 mass ascension process. Ascension to the mind is illogical. However, there will be no level of panic in anyone's mind that has become the violet energy force of Quantum Consciousness as gravity is neutralized.

Your souls have always energetically ascended back to the spiritual realm after the body they were in previously died. The completion of your soul's evolution is because you completed your activations of transformation. This will be the same ascension process that your soul has always known except this time it is extended to your body and mind because they too have become the violet energy force of Quantum Consciousness.

Your ascension also energetically transmutes your ascended self to become the absolute best you ever were while you were alive. Gone will be all pain. Gone will be all memories of suffering. Gone will be the ways of the physical world. Gone will be the energy of fear and negativity. Ascension begins God's ultimate energetic gift that has been pre-destined for your soul, body and mind before your soul transitioned back into the physical realm to begin its life experience as you.

Those who are the violet energy force of Quantum Consciousness will begin to lift off the ground effortlessly and ascend upward because the restraints of gravity will have been removed. You will peacefully and joyfully begin to see more of your physical surroundings. You will begin to ascend above the houses around you with absolutely no fear or mind limitations. Suddenly the houses from many streets over will begin to appear as you continue your ascension. As your ascension continues the outskirts and edges of your physical surroundings will begin to appear. Soon your town will disappear and all you see is the land mass from which you ascended from. Then in a flash earth will become a small dot. There will be no sensations other than absolute freedom and ecstasy during your ascension. Congratulations as you eternally unshackle the energetic restraints of the physical realm from your life.

Your ascension will be exactly the same as Jesus, Buddha, Moses and Elijah experienced as they too were energetically sealed by the violet energy force of God's Quantum Consciousness.

For the next 1000 years you and the ascended will become space travellers. You will travel to where no man has ever gone. It will be effortless as the violet energy force of Quantum Consciousness leads you in your travels throughout the Universe. There will be no need for food or water as there are no physical realm limitations. As the Quantum Consciousness of God you and everyone else who completed their activations of transformation will discover the miracles and marvels of the Universe and comprehend them from the perspective of God who created them.

Images from the Hubble Space Telescope estimate there are some 176 billion galaxies in our Universe. Imagine trying to see, learn and experience 176 billion galaxies in 1000 years, that's an average of 5 galaxies every second. Your 1000 year ascension will be energetically completed in a flash. It will be like a dream as you realize the incredible imagination that God created in every nook and cranny in the Universe.

However, back on earth during these same 1000 years it will be an entirely different story for the remaining souls who did not complete their activations of transformation.

I was impressed that while the ascended travel through the Universe on their 1000 year journey, the first piece of business back on earth for God will be to bind the Antichrist who God defeated in the energetic battle of Armageddon. This is confirmed in the bible's futuristic book of Revelation. It is found in Revelation 20:2-3 and reads, *"He seized the dragon, that ancient serpent, who is the devil, or Satan, and bound him for a thousand years. He threw him into the Abyss, and locked and sealed it over him, to keep him from deceiving the nations anymore until the thousand years were ended."*

The Antichrist will be energetically locked up and imprisoned for the same 1000 years that the ascended energetically travel throughout the Universe. This is to ensure that the Antichrist's dark force energy of fear and negativity cannot rear its ugly head during the 1000 years that energetically completes the energetic dilation of God's energetic pregnancy.

At this time back on Earth it will be in tatters. It will be chaotic and without structure. All of humanity's technology will have been rendered useless as there will be no electricity, no power, no tools and even no clothes for some. It will be like it was for the first humans except this time the remaining souls will carry with them the additional burden of not being able to get back to life as they know it can be. In their minds they will know where they came from and what they are missing, however, they will not have the ability to get back there.

The Quantum Consciousness of God will be starting humanity all over again from ground zero with the express purpose of re-activating its force of energetic perfection and perfect love sub atomically into the atoms of humanity's body and mind.

This civilization will start off far ahead of the first humans because they will carry with them the knowledge of life's potential and everything that has happened in the physical realm in the days that led up to the end of the 70 years of transformation and the 2082 ascension. As a result they will enjoy an accelerated evolution. Again the purpose of these souls who experience life during this time will be to complete their activations of transformation and re-activate their soul with the Quantum Consciousness of God.

I was inspired that the karma of the central bankers and their illuminati family who survived past December 21, 2082 will be paid back at this time. They will be left wondering what exactly happened because they thought they had life under control. For them they will be totally distraught and plagued with emotional and physical pain because of their pre ascension intent of purposely and knowingly placing humanity into energetic mind prisons for their personal gain.

The population at this time will be sparse in relationship to the seven billion plus souls that populated the world prior to the 2082 ascension. The Antichrist's dark force energy of fear and negativity will not be present on earth during these 1000 years as it remains locked up and away from the physical realm.

There will be two great cities in the world at this time. They will be for those who have chosen to complete their activations of transformation and become the Quantum Consciousness of God. During the 1000 years, if death happens to those who have completed their activations of transformation, their remains will be buried within the walls of the great city they occupied.

During the 1000 years there will be some who will not complete their activations of transformation. They will be scattered throughout the world and not be part of the two great cities. When they die, because their energy cannot be co-mingled with the Quantum Consciousness of God's energetic perfection and perfect love, their remains will be scattered throughout the world.

I was further impressed from the bible's futuristic book of Revelation in verse 20:7 what will happen at the end of the Antichrist's 1000 years of energetic incarceration. It reads *"When the thousand years are over, Satan will be released from his prison"*

When the Antichrist is released he will be full of rage and contempt as he unleashes his final attempt to prolong his survival. He will flatter all who are alive and have not completed their activations of transformation. The Antichrist will reveal to them secrets to protect themselves in the Antichrist's final attack against the souls who completed their activations of transformation in the two great cities. The Antichrist will attempt to wage a war against the two great cities and energetically lead those that did not complete their activations of transformation to attack the two great cities. When this happens the Quantum Consciousness of God will again energetically intervene to protect those who have been energetically sealed.

At this moment the final events on earth will take place to complete God's energetic dilation of its energetic pregnancy. Earth's second to last event was also described in the bible's futuristic book of Revelation verse 20:10

"And the devil, who deceived them, was thrown into the lake of burning sulphur ...will be tormented day and night for ever and ever." The Antichrist and all of its dark force energy of fear and negativity will finally be extinguished from the energetic fetus of

God as its purpose will have been served to help complete God's mastermind plan of life.

The eighth energy seal of Theta will then complete life on Earth with its final event. This will complete the energetic dilation in God's energetic pregnancy. Those who completed their activations of transformation between 2082 and 3082 will ascend and meet up with the ascended group of 2082. There will also be some souls who died before 3082. For these they will awaken and ascend with the surviving souls who completed their activations of transformation.

They will ascend and become one with the souls who ascended during the first mass ascension of 2082.

At this moment in time the Quantum Consciousness of God will also be energetically completing the same energetic event to the remaining life forms in all of its other 100 trillion energetic cells.

This will complete the Quantum Consciousness of God's Theta energy strand and the energetic dilation in God's energetic pregnancy. God's 100 trillion energetic cell fetus will now be ready to begin its energetic birth.

Part 5

The After Life

22

Forever

Next in God mastermind plan of life will be the energetic unlocking of God's ninth energy seal Iota. The energy released at the energetic unlocking of Iota is the energy that begins the energetic birth of God's 100 trillion energetic cell infinite, eternal energetic body on December 21, 3082.

I was inspired during my post NDE journey that our Universe is the lead energetic cell in God's 100 trillion cell infinite, eternal, energetic body. As the lead energetic cell, our Universe will be the first energetic cell to be energetically birthed through the sun onto the infinite, eternal energetic body of God.

Energetically, the birth of our Universe onto the infinite, eternal energetic body of God will have a couple of very different energetic forces attached to it that does not exist today in our physical realm. First all energy will be the Quantum Consciousness of God's energetic perfection and perfect love and and humanity will no longer be limited by the energetic confines of gravity. The body and minds of humanity will no longer be limited by gravity as they ascend onto God's infinite, eternal energetic body because they also are the violet energy Quantum Consciousness of God.

For the first time ever your soul will enter into its gravitational force still within you. It will be different this time as your soul has always only entered its gravitational force when it previously returned to the spiritual realm after leaving the physical realm either at the near death or death of the body it was previously in.

The energetic unlocking of God's tenth and final energy seal Omega accesses the limitless space travel potential of humanity into all other 100 trillion energetic cells of God. Omega completes the energetic birth of God's 100 trillion energetic cells onto the infinite, eternal energetic body of God. With the completion of Omega and the energetic birth of God's 100 trillion energetic cell infinite, eternal energetic body all energetic barriers that the Quantum Consciousness of God had put in place to deny any of its 100 trillion energetic cells from contacting each other during the 13.75 billion year energetic gestation will be gone.

The ascended from the first and second ascensions will live eternally as the violet energy energetic perfection and perfect love of God. They will now have energetically transitioned out of God's energetic fetus because they have become the violet energy Quantum Consciousness of God. As the energetic perfection and perfect love of God your energetic play land will be the 100 trillion energetic cells of God's infinite, eternal energetic body. No longer will you be confined by gravity to just one place in one cell. As the violet energy Quantum Consciousness of God your home will be God's 100 trillion energetic cell body of infinite possibility.

There will be a limitless amount of life forms in God's 100 trillion energetic cell infinite, eternal energetic body and all will be the Quantum Consciousness of God's imagination that will make up the 100 trillion violet energy cells.

Imagine what your first encounter with a violet energy alien life form from another energetic cell will be like. Imagine what your first glimpse into an alien violet energy cell will reveal. The possibilities are infinite and limitless. There will be no energy of fear or negativity to hold you back from discovering the splendor and magnificence of God's Quantum Consciousness. It will only be the energetic Quantum Consciousness of God's energetic perfection and perfect love that exists.

This is and always has been God's ultimate wisdom for life that has been energetically programmed into his mastermind plan of life. This is the Quantum Consciousness of life. The Quantum Consciousness violet energy force of God will be wherever we go, with whomever or whatever we meet at every second of every moment forever.

All pain and suffering your soul has ever had to endure in the physical realm was part of God's mastermind plan of life so that his utopian wonderland of energetic perfection and perfect love could include your very best self in it.

Of all the mammals, humanity is the only one that is cruel and the only one that inflicts pain for the pleasure of doing it. Fortunately, the traits of humanity and ego will not exist in God's infinite, eternal energetic body of violet energy energetic perfection and perfect love.

PART 6

The Choice

23

The Crossroads of Time

"The mind is everything, what you think you become."

Buddha

I was impressed during my post NDE journey that the cross over energy between knowledge for our mind and wisdom for our soul is love.

It is because of the Quantum Consciousness of God's energetic pulse of energy that your mind, body and soul has been brought to your cross roads of time. Which energetic pathway will your mind choose to go down? It's only you that can make this choice.

God's mastermind plan of life was created so that your mind would choose the energetic pathway that it deems is right for you.

Will your mind choose the pathway that transforms you into the Quantum Consciousness of God or will it choose the pathway that does not transform you into the Quantum Consciousness of God?

Will your mind choose to become the Quantum Consciousness of God and live forever in its superhuman state or will it choose death, destruction and decay that satisfies your ego because you chose to be a slave to money?

It's only you that can choose.

I am forever reminded about the story of one of my friends whose activations of transformation I had the pleasure of completing. Her name is Anna.

Anna grew up an atheist. Anna remembered as a child not being able to express her feelings or emotions, only facts. Anna had 3 older siblings who were all quite a bit older than she was. Growing up Anna was never accepted by her father and was always told she fell short of her older siblings accomplishments.

From childhood Anna realized her best option for survival was not to have a relationship with her father, and this was fine with him.

Soon after Anna completed her activations of transformation she spoke with her sister who told her their father had been diagnosed with pancreatic cancer and the prognosis was not good. His health was deteriorating rapidly and it was only a matter of days that he had left to live.

Anna knew she had to put her past feelings and resentment towards her father behind her and she unconditionally forgave him. This was not easy for Anna to do; however, she was able to go into the final meeting with her father with a clean slate because she forgave him.

When Anna walked into his hospital room she saw only a skeleton of the man she had last seen so many years before. Anna remembered the puzzled look on his face when he saw her.

At this moment Anna realized she wanted to inspire her father's soul but had no idea how. Then suddenly, after exchanging pleasantries, the needed words just poured out of her mouth. Anna asked her father if he had any questions about the journey he was about to take. Anna remembers that upon hearing this question a glow and smile appeared on her father's face she never remembered seeing before.

Anna told her father about the journey his soul was about to take and that very soon he would simply just fall asleep and the journey would begin. Upon hearing this he apologized to Anna for how he had treated her as a child. He asked for her forgiveness and thanked her for the information regarding the journey he was about to take.

By this time, Anna could see her father was having a difficult time staying awake and Anna gave him one final kiss on his forehead and said goodbye. When Anna looked back at her father one final time she remembered a peace on his face she had never seen before.

Anna's father died shortly after her visit and his soul transitioned back to the spiritual realm. He did not hear about how he could transform the force of God nor did he know about activations of transformation. Anna knows her father's soul has returned back to the spiritual realm to prepare itself for his soul's final life experience which may or may not have already begun in the physical realm.

There are many souls who have died before and after December 21, 2012 whose soul has yet to awaken in the physical realm to unleash their Quantum Consciousness of God limitless potential. Please know that these souls's final life experience is either happening again right now or will happen very soon.

Up until December 21, 2012 at 11:11:11 GMT, the Quantum Consciousness of God had purposely been separated from the physical realm to complete the energetic gestation of its energetic fetus. Up until December 21, 2012 at 11:11:11 GMT only violet energy threads of God's Quantum Consciousness were in the physical realm while its energetic fetus was gestating. The violet energy threads of God's Quantum Consciousness that were in the

Universe while God's energetic fetus completed its gestation was the souls of humanity.

The Quantum Consciousness of God has always energetically communicated with every atom in the Universe through its energetic pulse of energy. This was to ensure the completion of its energetic fetus's gestation and the completion of its mastermind plan of life.

The Quantum Consciousness of God's energetic perfection and perfect love begins and ends with its mastermind plan of life. Life has been maintained by energy, the energetic pulse and regulator for Quantum Consciousness to every atom in the Universe through its energetic superstrings. Energy has been the Quantum Consciousness of God's energetic pulse that energetically communicated through its energy superstrings. Energy has always adhered to God's mastermind plan of life.

God's mastermind plan of life is now at its crossroads of time, the energetic battle of Armageddon, when it's most important step can either be completed or not be completed. God has left it to your mind to decide what road time will travel down. God's energetic fetus of life will either be birthed or aborted and it's your mind that helps create the outcome.

The reason and purpose I returned from my June 25, 1996 death was to reveal the Quantum Consciousness of God and awaken the souls of humanity so that life could be re-energized as the violet energy force of God's Quantum Consciousness.

Every soul is here on this planet right now for this to happen. Everyone is alive today to activate and unleash their super human energetic potential of ultimate wisdom for their soul, ultimate wellness for their body and ultimate wealth for their mind.

Everyone is alive today so their body and minds atoms can be sub atomically transfigured into the violet energy of God's Quantum Consciousness to ensure that their ticket has been punched for the December 21, 2082 ascension. This will complete everyone's soul evolution and unleash their limitless potential.

Everyone is alive today so that their body and mind can be energtically transfigured into the absolute best it has ever been as the energetic perfection and perfect love of God's violet energy Quantum Consciousness.

Imagine the possibilities for life without the Antichrist's dark force energy of fear and negativity.

Imagine the possibilities when you become the Quantum Consciousness of God and your state of super humanity begins to be activated and unleashed in you.

Imagine the possibilities when 144,000 likeminded individuals have all completed their activations of transformation and the energetic disposition of humanity instantly changes to soul, body and mind and ego is eliminated.

Imagine the possibilities when money is energetically led by the Quantum Consciousness of God.

Imagine the possibilities when all of your atoms are transfigured sub atomically into the violet energy force of God's Quantum Consciousness.

The possibilities are infinite.

Awakening your soul and unleashing the Quantum Consciousness of God's violet energy force into your body and mind is why your soul came back for its final life experience. It's also why your soul has had all of its previous life experiences so that it can be successful in this life experience through you to complete its evolution. You are what your soul has always known it would become.

Unleashing your limitless potential and Quantum Consciousness through you is your souls' ultimate purpose and mission that completes its evolution and births the infinite, eternal, energetic body of God. Your soul has always been learning in all of its past life experiences to energetically perfect itself through you in this life experience to complete this mission.

The purpose of your soul's present life experience is to complete its evolution by unleashing your limitless potential and Quantum Consciousness of God sub atomically into every atom of who you are. This will complete your soul's lifelong evolution. Your soul has always known it will activate and unleash the Quantum Consciousness of God's energetic perfection and perfect love sub atomically to your body and mind atoms to ascend onto God's infinite, eternal, energetic body of life.

As the violet energy Quantum Consciousness of God is reactivated with your soul it produces an overpowering gut feeling of excitement and joy that bubbles up within you. This is your soul's energetic signal that it is awakening to fulfill its lifelong purpose and mission that all of its past life experiences have contributed towards completing.

God's mastermind plan of life is now delivering God's fully developed energetic fetus and the completion of your soul's evolution is an integral part of this energetic delivery. Your soul is an energetic obstetrician in the energetic birth of God.

The Quantum Consciousness of God has been revealed at this moment in time to complete God's energetic pregnancy of life. It has been revealed because your body and mind is an essential component in this process.

The admission price onto God's infinite, eternal, energetic body of life is the reactivation of your soul with the Quantum Consciousness of God. Your transformation and transfiguration into the Quantum Consciousness of God completes your soul's evolution and punches your ticket onto God's infinite, eternal energetic body.

What always astounds me about the Quantum Consciousness of God is how the most important step has been left to our minds. Completing God's energetic perfection and perfect love produces His infinite, eternal, energetic body of life and it's our minds that will establish it.

Consider this your RSVP to attend God's party of life on His infinite, eternal energetic body.

No matter what you choose, it is what your mind has deemed is best for you. Your mind has only two choices, either Edge God Out or Let God In.

This concludes the reason why life is and your choice in it.

Please feel free to email me at info@awakentheforce.org any time regarding the art of awakening the force and Quantum Consciousness of God within you to unleash your limitless potential. I look forward to your email.

Enjoy the journey!

Glossary

10 energy seals- these are the God's energetic figures of attestation and authenticity on his Energetic Blueprint of life. When energetically unlocked they release the violet energy strands that make up the violet energy totality and Quantum Consciousness of God's violet energy force.

10 wisdoms for the soul- they are inspiration, love, hope, discernment, instinct, intuition, insight, coincidence, déjà vu and imagination.

70 year transformation- this began on December 21, 2012 at 11:11:13 GMT at the energetic unlocking of the seventh energy seal Eta on God's violet energy mastermind plan of life. It signals the beginning of the energetic battle of Armageddon on earth within the minds of humanity.

Activations of transformation –this is how God's violet energy Quantum Consciousness re-activates itself with your soul in the physical realm. When completed your body and minds atoms are transfigured into violet energy Quantum Consciousness of God.

Alpha energy seal- this was the Quantum Consciousness of God's first energy seal that was energetically unlocked on God's Energetic Blueprint of life 13.75 billion years ago.

Glossary

Antichrist- this is the energy of concentrated evil that was released by the pale lightning bolt and the Quantum Consciousness of God during the energetic unlocking of the fourth energy seal 13.75 billion years ago. The energetic role of the Antichrist in God's violet energy Quantum Consciousness was to act as the "devil's advocate "in life. It gave humanity a choice to either become the Quantum Consciousness of God or to be led by the energy of the Antichrist. If the Antichrist's dark force energy of fear and negativity had not existed there would be no free will choice by humanity to become the Quantum Consciousness of God's energetic perfection and perfect love. The release of the Antichrist and its dark force energy was part of the Quantum Consciousness of God's energetic perfection and perfect love. Without the antichrist humanity could not have chosen to become the Quantum Consciousness of God.

Ascension- this is the event that transitions humanity's mind, body and soul out of God's energetic fetus and into God's infinite, eternal energetic body.

Beta brainwave speed-this is the speed at which our minds process life at (14-39 cycles per second) in the physical realm.

Beta energy seal- this was the second energy seal that was energetically unlocked on God's Energetic Blueprint of life. It was energetically unlocked 13.75 billion years ago; 1 second after the Alpha energy seal was energetically unlocked.

Glossary

Birth portal- this is the Quantum Consciousness of God's first energetic portal I saw during my NDE after God energetically unlocked its Gamma energy seal from its Energetic Blueprint of life. It is the energetic portal where God's energetic threads of Quantum Consciousness or our souls transition through as they leave the spiritual realm and enter the physical realm to begin their next life experience.

Black force energy- this is the energy that the Quantum Consciousness of God unleashed at the opening of its third energy seal. Science refers to this energy as the gravitational force or gravity.

Collective unconsciousness- this is the energetic mind of the soul. It produces the 4 traits of a person's personality. The 4 traits of a person's personality are security, sexuality, identity and spirituality. It also created our brainstem and brain after conception.

Death portal- this is the second energetic portal I saw during my NDE when God energetically unlocked its Gamma energy seal on its Energetic Blueprint of life. It is the energetic portal that energetic threads of God's Quantum Consciousness transition through as they leave the physical realm after the death of the body they had experienced life in. This is the portal our souls go through to return to the spiritual realm after the body they resided in died.

Glossary

Delta energy seal- this was the Quantum Consciousness of God's fourth energy seal that was energetically unlocked on the Energetic Blueprint of life. It was energetically unlocked 13.75 billion years ago, 3 seconds after its Alpha energy seal was energetically unlocked, 2 seconds after its Beta energy seal was energetically unlocked and 1 second after its Gamma energy seal was energetically unlocked.

Divine Aid Philanthropists- this is what those who have completed their activations of transformation and completed their function in the Spiritual Awakening Strategy (SAS) become. Their super human ultimate wealth will fund the divine requirements and needs of God's Quantum Consciousness in the energetic battle of Armageddon. Through the initiatives of God, for the public good they financially help to energetically defeat the dark force energy of fear and negativity.

Divine Aid Philanthropy- this is the fulfilling of the Quantum Consciousness of God's requirements and needs during the energetic battle of Armageddon. It will help to defeat the Antichrist in the energetic battle of Armageddon.

Electromagnetic force of nature- this is the Quantum Consciousness of God's red force energy unleashed at the opening of its Beta energy seal.

Glossary

Energetic battle of Armageddon- this is the final battle between the energies of good and the energies of evil in the physical realm. It pits the Antichrist's dark force energy of fear and negativity against God's Quantum Consciousness violet energy force of energetic perfection and perfect love. This energetic battle of Armageddon began within the minds of humanity on December 21, 2012 at 11:11:11 GMT when the violet energy Quantum Consciousness of God energetically unlocked its Epsilon energy seal on its Energetic Blueprint of life.

Energetic birth- this is the energetic birth of God's 100 trillion energetic cell fetus that begins with the energetic unlocking of God's Iota energy seal and concludes at the completion of the Quantum Consciousness of God's Omega violet energy strand.

Energetic Blueprint of life- this is the energetic signature of God that is the foundation of God's violet energy Quantum Consciousness and the energetic foundation of every atom in the Universe.

Energetic breaking of water- this was the energetic event during God's energetic pregnancy that occurred on December 21, 2012 at 11:11:11 GMT when the fifth energetic seal, Epsilon was energetically unlocked. It was the moment in time when the violet energy Quantum Consciousness of God transitioned out of the spiritual realm and entered the physical realm to begin the energetic delivery of God's 100 trillion energetic cell fetus.

Glossary

Energetic conception- this was the energetic event unleashed by the energetic unlocking of the Alpha energy seal on God's Energetic Blueprint of life, 13.75 billion years ago.

Energetic dilation- this is and will be the energetic events that have and will unleash the energetic beginning, continuance and completion of the energetic dilation of God's energetic pregnancy. The beginning energy for the energetic dilation was unleashed at the opening of Zeta energy seal on December 21, 2012 at 11:11:12 GMT. The continuance energy for the energetic dilation was unleashed at the opening of the Eta energy seal on December 21, 2012 at 11:11:13 GMT. The completion energy will be unleashed at the opening of God's Theta energy seal from His Energetic Blueprint of life on December 21, 2082 at 11:11:13 GMT.

Energetic disposition- this is and has been the energetic order of humanity's 3 components of mind, body and soul. Until this final life experience for your soul a person's energetic disposition has always been energetically wired this way for survival. However in this your soul's final life experience your soul's purpose and mission is to activate its active lead role through you and change your energetic disposition from mind, body and soul to soul, body and mind so that your limitless potential and the Quantum Consciousness of God can be unleashed through you.

Energetic fetus- this energetically resides in God's energetic womb. It is made up of 100 trillion energetic cells of which our Universe is God's lead energetic cell.

Energetic gestation- this was the energetic events that were unleashed at the opening of the Beta, Gamma and Delta energy seals that began, continued and endured the energetic gestation of God's energetic fetus. Energetic gestation of the energetic fetus began 13.75 billion years ago and ended on December 21, 2012 at 11:11:11 GMT with the opening of the Epsilon energy seal.

Energetic hub- this is God in the energetic wheel of spirituality.

Energetic mind prison- this is where the minds of humanity have been placed because of the controlling and manipulative dark force fear and negativity energy of the Antichrist. The minds of humanity are kept in the Antichrist's energetic mind prison by satisfying the minds ego through money that temporarily soothes the egos fear and insecurity.

Energetic parasite- these are energetic organisms that have been found to reside within a person's soul. They enter a soul to spy on what is energetically happening in our Universe. They are energies from other energetic cells and/or other galaxies from within our Universe. When found during activations of transformation they are always removed and returned back to the energetic location they came from.

Glossary

Energetic pregnancy- this is what the Quantum Consciousness of God is in the midst of completing. It began with the energetic conception of His energetic fetus 13.75 billion years ago and will conclude with the birth of His 100 trillion energetic cell infinite, eternal, energetic body of violet energy energetic perfection and perfect love.

Energetic spokes- these are the different faiths, religions and spiritual movements that connect or point to the energetic hub of God on the energetic wheel of spirituality. They energetically link with humanity. Their main purpose has been to keep humanity from annihilating themselves.

Energetic tipping point- this is the point in time when 144,000 individuals will have completed their activations of transformation to re-activate their soul with the Quantum Consciousness of God.

Energetic wheel of spirituality- the energetic wheel of spirituality consists of its energetic wheel of humanity, its energetic hub of God and its energetic spokes of faith that connect the energetic hub of God with the energetic wheel of humanity.

Energy- this is the Quantum Consciousness of God's right hand and energetic pulse that is regulating God's mastermind plan of life to its conclusion.

Energy of fear and negativity- this is the dark force energy of the Antichrist that keeps humanity trapped in the Antichrist's energetic mind prison. It is this energy that keeps the illusion of life alive by feeding humanity their drug of money to temporarily soothe their mind's ego.

Energy zings- these are what I experienced during my NDE. They were from the Quantum Consciousness of God's violet energy communication to me during my June 25, 1996 NDE.

Epsilon energy seal- this was the Quantum Consciousness of God's fifth energy seal that was energetically unlocked on the Energetic Blueprint of life on December 21, 2012 at 11:11:11 GMT.

Eta energy seal- this was the Quantum Consciousness of God's seventh energy seal that was energetically unlocked on the Energetic Blueprint of life on December 21, 2012 at 11:11:13 GMT.

Faith- this is a confidence, trust or belief in the existence of God without any proof. The primary purpose of faith during the gestation of God's energetic fetus was to keep humanity from annihilating themselves.

First time soul- this is a collective unconsciousness and soul that energetically resides in a person that is making its first life experience into the physical realm.

Glossary

Force- this is God's violet energy Quantum Consciousness.

Gamma energy seal- this was the Quantum Consciousness of God's third energy seal that was energetically unlocked on the Energetic Blueprint of life 13.75 billion years ago, 2 seconds after the Alpha energy seal was energetically unlocked and 1 second after the Beta energy seal was energetically unlocked.

God- this is the energetic architect of life who through his minds Quantum Consciousness is completing his energetic mastermind plan of life.

God's energetic cells- this is all of God's 100 trillion energetic cells of His energetic fetus of which our Universe is the lead energetic cell. They will be energetically birthed to create God's 100 trillion energetic cell infinite, eternal, energetic body of energetic perfection and perfect love.

God's energetic threads- these are our souls.

God's energetic womb- this is where God's energetic fetus of life energetically resides. It also was my energetic screen during my NDE that revealed the energetic events that has and will take place within it. It is the female component of God and the place where everything the male component of God has thought into existence.

God's portal- this was the fourth energetic portal I saw during the energetic unlocking of the Gamma energy seal from the Energetic

Blueprint of life. It also is the energetic portal the violet energy Quantum Consciousness of God transitioned through on December 21, 2012 at 11:11:11 GMT to leave the spiritual realm and enter the physical realm.

Gravitational force of nature- this is the Quantum Consciousness of God's black force energy that was unleashed at the opening of the Gamma energy seal, 13.75 billion years ago.

Illusion- this is humanity's everyday impression of reality that their minds perceive to be real. It has been created by the Illusionist and allowed to flourish by the Antichrist. It has trapped the minds of humanity in the Antichrist's energetic mind prisons through the energy of fear and negativity. When chosen as a person's ultimate energy it means a person's mind has chosen to not become the Quantum Consciousness of God and to not be transformed and transfigured into God's violet energy Quantum Consciousness of energetic perfection and perfect love.

Illusionist- this is the physical entities that control the central bank's global monetization policies and matrix. They have made themselves invisible yet exercise the Antichrist's power from behind the scenes on everything to trap humanity in the Antichrist's energetic mind prisons.

Glossary

Infinite, eternal, energetic body of God- this will be the energetic end result of God's energetic mastermind plan of life. It is why life exists.

Iota energy seal- this is the Quantum Consciousness of God's ninth energy seal that will be energetically unlocked on the Energetic Blueprint of life on December 21, 3082 at 11:11:13 GMT.

Last time soul- this is a soul who is in the physical realm for its final life experience.

Life- this is the energetic fetus of God and will be energetically birthed to become the infinite, eternal energetic body of God.

Life energy- this is a soul and energetic thread of God's violet energy Quantum Consciousness.

Life energy contract- these are the energetic parameters for each soul's next physical realm life experience. Life energy contracts build upon a soul's previous life energy contract towards its final physical realm life experience. The purpose of life energy contracts is to provide the soul with its energetic parameters for its next life experience in the physical realm. All life energy contracts are completed with the Quantum Consciousness of God in the spiritual realm before the soul transitions back to the physical realm for their next life experience.

Limitless potential- this is the energetic aspect of God's Quantum Consciousness that is transformed through you after completing your activations of transformation. It is the Quantum Consciousness of God's potential for your life. It will transfigure your body and minds atoms sub atomically into the violet energy Quantum Consciousness of God. It also will activate your state of super humanity until your ascension onto God's infinite, eternal energetic body.

Love triangle- these are energetic triangles between the Quantum Consciousness of God, your soul and anything else that your prayer or meditation places into the Quantum Consciousness of God. The purpose of love triangles is to energetically transfigure every atom of the Universe into the violet energy Quantum Consciousness of God.

Messiah- this is a spiritual term that refers to the violet energy Quantum Consciousness of God.

Middle aged soul - this is the collective unconsciousness and soul age of a soul that resides in a person based on the number of previous life experiences it has had in the physical realm.

Money- money is the commodity of the illusionist. It is his drug for humanity. It is the drug humanity requires to satisfy their ego. The younger a soul is the more its ego needs money and the tougher it will be for this person to complete their activations of transformation. Money will ultimately become the violet energy currency of God. God's Quantum Consciousness will eliminate the Antichrist's dark force of fear and negativity from money.

Near Death Experience (NDE)-this is the term used to describe an experience of the soul. NDE's are when the soul leaves the physical body and energetically travels to the spiritual realm through their near death portal to have a One-on-One energetic encounter with the Quantum Consciousness of God. During this encounter, the Quantum Consciousness of God energetically notifies the soul that it must return to their physical body to get back on track and fulfill its life energy contract that it has strayed away from while doing life. NDE's happen so that the soul can get back on course to fulfill their purpose and mission in their life experience.

Near Death Portal- this is the third energetic portal I saw during my NDE when the Gamma energy seal was energetically unlocked. It is the energetic portal that God's energetic threads of Quantum Consciousness or souls transition through as they leave the physical realm after the person they have resided in suffers a near death. The soul returns back to the spiritual realm for its energetic meeting with the Quantum Consciousness of God to get back on track in their life experience.

Glossary

Old soul-this is a collective unconsciousness and soul that due to the amount of previous life experiences it has can be identified as old.

Omega energy seal- this is the Quantum Consciousness of God's tenth and final energy seal that will be energetically unlocked on the Energetic Blueprint of life at a time that is only known by the Quantum Consciousness of God after December 21, 3082. It completes the energetic birth of God's 100 trillion energetic cell infinite, eternal energetic body.

Pale force energy- this is the energy unleashed at the energetic unlocking of the Quantum Consciousness of God's fourth energy seal, Delta. Science has identified this energy as the weak force of nature.

Perfect Love- this is what energy is in God's energetic mastermind plan of life.

Physical realm- this is the reality our 5 senses of sight, sound, taste, touch and smell understands and interprets as reality through our Beta brainwave processing speed of 14-39 cycles per second.

Quantum Consciousness- this is what God's thoughts are.

Red force energy- this is the energy unleashed at the energetic unlocking of God's second energy seal, Beta. Science has identified this energy as the electromagnetic force of nature.

Glossary

Soul Awakening Strategy (SAS)- this is the strategic game plan that will re-energize money through the Quantum Consciousness of God's energetic perfection and perfect love to defeat the dark force energy of the Antichrist in the energetic battle of Armageddon.

Spiritual realm- this is the realm where the Quantum Consciousness of God's violet energy force resided until December 21, 2012 at 11:11:11 GMT.

Stress- Stress is produced by the Antichrist's energy of fear and negativity. It leads to aging, age related disease and ultimately death to the physical body and mind.

Strong force of nature- this is the Quantum Consciousness of God's white force energy unleashed at the opening of the first energy seal, 13.75 billion years ago.

Super humanity- this will be the Quantum Consciousness of God's temporary bionic state of energetic perfection for humanity in the physical realm. It unleashes the Quantum Consciousness of God's ultimate wisdom for the soul, the Quantum Consciousness of God's ultimate wellness for the body and the Quantum Consciousness of God's ultimate wealth for the mind.

The Sealing- this re-activates the violet energy Quantum Consciousness of God within a person to unleash their limitless potential. The sealing begins when a person completes their activation of transformation which reactivates God's violet energy Quantum Consciousness totality with their soul. The violet energy Quantum Consciousness of God acts as the restoring force to transfigure a person's atoms sub atomically from their red, green and blue energy to the violet energy Quantum Consciousness of God. As more violet energy is sub atomically transfigured a person begins to unleash their state of super humanity. Super humanity is a person's ultimate wisdom for their soul, ultimate wellness for their body and ultimate wealth for their mind. The sealing's final benefit is its body, mind and souls ascension onto the infinite, eternal, energetic body of God.

Theta brainwave speed- this is the speed your mind (4-8 cycles per second) comprehends God's energetic communications at. It is also your minds speed at which a person completes their activations of transformation.

Theta energy seal- this is the Quantum Consciousness of God's eighth energy seal that will be energetically unlocked on God's Energetic Blueprint of life on December 21, 2082 at 11:11:13 GMT.

Transfiguration- this is the subatomic energetic process that converts humanity's red, green and blue sub atomic energy into its violet energy Quantum Consciousness of God.

Glossary

Prior to my NDE, it had been completed 4 times in the history of humanity to Jesus, Buddha, Moses and Elijah.

Violet energy- this is the Quantum Consciousness of God. It is the God's energetic mastermind plan of life.

The foundation of violet energy is the ten energetic seals of its Energetic Blueprint of life. They were energetically unlocked to unleash their ten strands of violet energy that in their totality make up the totality of violet energy.

Violet energy is the energetic perfection and perfect love of God.

Violet sun- this is the violet energy Quantum Consciousness of God I saw during my NDE after the second energy seal was energetically unlocked.

Weak force of nature- this is the Quantum Consciousness of God's pale force energy that was unleashed at the opening of the Delta energy seal.

White force energy- this is the energy unleashed at the energetic unlocking of the Quantum Consciousness of God's first energy seal, Alpha. Science has identified this energy as the strong force of nature.

Young soul- this is a collective unconsciousness and soul that due to the amount of previous life experiences can be identified as young.

Zeta energy seal- this was the Quantum Consciousness of God's sixth energy seal that was energetically unlocked on the Energetic Blueprint of life on December 21, 2012 at 11:11:12 GMT.

Made in the USA
Charleston, SC
06 January 2015